Metaphysical
Horror

Metaphysical Horror

Leszek Kolakowski

Basil Blackwell

First published 1988
Reprinted 1988

Basil Blackwell Ltd
108 Cowley Road, Oxford OX4 1JF, UK

Basil Blackwell Inc.
432 Park Avenue South, Suite 1503
New York, NY 10016, USA

British Library Cataloguing in Publication Data

Kolakowski, Leszek
Metaphysical horror.
1. Metaphysics
1. Title
110   B945.K7/
ISBN 0-631-15959-2

Library of Congress Cataloging in Publication Data

Kolakowski, Leszek.
Metaphysical horror / Leszek Kolakowski.
p. cm.
Includes index.
ISBN 0-631-15959-2
1. Metaphysics. 2. Philosophy. I. Title.
B4691.K5863M47   1988
190—dc19

Typeset in 12 on 14pt Garamond
by DMB (Typesetting), Abingdon, Oxon.
Printed in Great Britain
by Billing and Sons Ltd, Worcester

Contents

Contents

Metaphysical
Horror

ON PHILOSOPHERS

A modern philosopher who has never experienced the
feeling of being a charlatan is such a shallow mind that his
work is probably not worth reading.

For centuries philosophy asserted its legitimacy by
asking and answering questions it had inherited from the
Socratic and pre-Socratic legacy, that is, how to distinguish the real from the unreal, the true from the false,
the good from the evil. There is one man with whom all
European philosophers identify themselves, even if they
dismiss his ideas altogether. This is Socrates – a philosopher who is unable to identify himself with this
archetypal figure does not belong to this civilization.

ON PHILOSOPHY

At a certain moment, however, philosophers had to face,
and to cope with, a simple, painfully undeniable fact:
among questions that have sustained the life of European
philosophy for two and a half millennia not a single one has

1

ever been solved to our general satisfaction; all of them remain either controversial or invalidated by philosophers' decree. To be a nominalist or anti-nominalist is culturally and intellectually as possible today as it was in the twelfth century; to believe or not to believe that one may tell phenomena from the essence is as admissible as it used to be in ancient Greece; and so is to think that the distinction between good and evil is a contingent convention or that it is embedded in the order of things. You may still be a respectable person whether you believe or refuse to believe in God; no standards in our civilization prevent you from thinking that language reflects reality or that it creates it; and you are not barred from good society if you accept or dismiss the semantic concept of truth. Whatever matters in philosophy – and this means: whatever makes philosophy matter at all in life – is subject to the same options that have persisted since the unidentifiable moment when independent thought, disregarding the mythological legacy as a source of authority, arose in our civilization. The vocabulary and the forms of expression have changed, to be sure, and many mutations have occurred – thanks to the number of great minds who appear occasionally in every century – yet the kernel which keeps philosophy alive is unchanged.

ON PHILOSOPHY'S SELF-MARTYRDOM

Various strategies have been devised to deal with this apparently self-defeating status of philosophy. The least reliable but the most successful, at least in terms of a philosopher's self-confidence, consists in denying that the situation just described obtains at all. Some questions are declared meaningless and thus non-questions; the meaningful ones are soluble, not unlike scientific problems, and many have actually been solved – if some people are not ready to accept the solution, they only thereby display their intellectual ineptitude. Die-hard analytical philosophers and old-style phenomenologists who openly philosophize within the framework of this strategy are now, however numerous, endangered species.

The second strategy embraces a variety of relativistic ways out. The meaning of philosophical questions, like all others, is defined either by the rules of a linguistic game or by a historical setting, a specific civilization within which they were uttered, or else by the considerations of usefulness. There are no obligatory standards of rationality and therefore there is no such thing as validity *tout court*. A philosophical truth, a solution of the problem may indeed be valid but, if so, it is valid in relation to a game, a culture or a collective or individual goal. We simply cannot go any further, we have no tools to force the door leading us beyond language, beyond a set of contingent cultural norms or beyond practical imperatives which mould our thinking process.

There are two basic interpretations of this relativistic approach: latitudinarian-anarchist and restrictive. In the former, anything goes that is admissible or good (linguistically, culturally, practically); the difference between, say, believing and not believing in the Devil is similar to the difference between a vegetarian and a meat-eater or between monogamous and polygamous social orders. Some cultures, or some games, may forbid or impose belief in the Devil, some prescribe dietary norms, some do not. If the language of the culture I am an inhabitant of allows for both vegetarian and non-vegetarian diets, I am right in either choice on the assumption that it serves me well, and the same applies to belief or disbelief in the

3

Devil. If a society imposes monogamy on its members, and survives, monogamy is right and thus true: at any rate scientific, philosophical and religious beliefs enjoy no other kind of truth. Rules come first, reality hinges on them. God does not exist in Albania, but he very much does in Persia; Heisenberg's principle is valid now but was not in ancient Athens.

The trouble with this generous interpretation of relativism is that although it might satisfy some philosophers, it appears poorly designed when confronted with the inveterate (albeit regrettable, in their view) mental customs of mankind, including scientists. Conforming with these customs, when I say 'the Devil tempted me', I mean that the Devil tempted me. A linguistic, historical or utilitarian relativism allows for a set of rules within which it is permissible to say 'the Devil tempted me', but when saying so I am supposed to mean precisely that: 'it is permissible according to the rules I live by to say "the Devil tempted me"' (or to say 'the sum of three angles of any triangle is equal to two right angles'). In other words, I have to obey a rule ordering me to keep in mind that whatever I am saying I am not saying that something is the case but that – nothing being the case – the rules give me the right to say so: this amounts to stating that we all ought to speak only in a kind of metalanguage. Thus phrased, this prescription might sound wierd, but I do not see how a generous relativism could avoid it without being suspected of falling into the rationalist prejudices of old. Assuming, for the sake of argument, that the prescription can be both uttered and applied consistently, it is obviously at odds with the dominant rules of speaking. The question is: why should the prevailing rules be abrogated in favour of the relativistic ones? If the rule about the relativity of rules is not supposed to be relative itself, it is bound to be an arbitrary decree, and if it is as relative as the rules to which it applies, it has no more force than the opposite one and the statement 'nothing is the case' is in no better position than 'it is not true that nothing is the case.' And it should be observed that both statements 'nothing is the case' and 'it is not true that nothing is the case' are not uttered in a metalanguage.

The Wittgensteinian solution is probably the only reliable and consistent way of unknotting the dilemma. It goes further in self-interpretation. When I am talking about the relativity of knowledge I emit meaningless sounds and am not supposed to say anything true or false. My words, without carrying any cognitive power, have a therapeutic value, however, insofar as they help me and you to be relieved from philosophical problems, including in particular the problem of the relativity of knowledge and the self-reference paradox which it entails. And this seems to boil down to a piece of practical advice: stop bothering yourself about philosophy and if the misfortune of being a philosopher does befall you, you had better look for a more respectable job and become a nurse, a priest, a plumber or a circus clown; in those areas of activity people understand each other fairly well without asking impossible epistemological questions. Wittgenstein himself apparently tried, but failed consistently to follow, this sensible exhortation (though he did not phrase it, to be fair) and it does not seem to be frequently repeated or voiced aloud by those whose intellectual manners have been fashioned by his words.

Restrictive relativism is less consistent in that it accepts the culture-bound or language-bound or pragmatic character of 'truth' but it invalidates in advance metaphysical curiosity, that is to say, it makes illicit all questions about what is or is not 'real'. And yet, if we are

consistent in our relativism, there is no point in distinguishing between metaphysical and empirical questions
and no reason why the question about the truth of the
great Fermat's theorem should be legitimate in contrast
to the question, say, about how Jesus Christ's body is
present in the Eucharist. The only legitimacy conceivable
is related to the established standards of a culture or a
language and the validity of a question – about Fermat's
theorem or the Eucharist – is defined by the rules of a
particular game, whether those rules give voice to a
particular sensitivity of a civilization, or have been
established arbitrarily. We cannot make a set of questions
permanently invalid unless we implicitly appeal to the
permanent standards of rationality.

It was known to the ancient sceptics and it has been
known ever since that any epistemology, that is, any
attempt to build universal criteria of validity for
knowledge, leads either to an infinite regression or to a
vicious circle or to an invincible self-reference paradox
(invincible, that is, unless it is spuriously solved by being
converted into an infinite regression). The most vexing
side of this old insight consists in that once it is stated it
falls prey to its own verdict, which means that a sceptic is
inconsistent by the very fact of preaching the sceptical
doctrine. Thus far, the (early) Wittgenstein seems to be
vindicated.

Moreover, the relativist doctrine, apart from being
incapable of finding consistent means of self-expression, is
inconsistent insofar as it implicitly admits – as invariably
happens – the very principle of consistency. Universal
relativism usually spares logic; not surprisingly, since to
proclaim that the rule of non-contradiction is valid only
within the limits of a language game or of a civilization
makes further communication impracticable and leaves

relativism in a state of self-inflicted paralysis. The most implacable relativism leaves the validity of the rule of non-contradiction untouched, thereby surreptitiously admitting some eternal (or at least non-historical and not confined to a linguistic game) norms of rationality. Universal relativism usually spares mathematics, too. It is easier to follow the leaps in the history of empirical sciences and humanities than to answer the simple question: how did it happen that Galileo and Newton left Aristotelian physics in a shambles whereas Euclid's proofs are still valid?

ITS SELF-DERISION

For well over a hundred years, a large portion of academic philosophy has been devoted to explaining that philosophy is either impossible or useless or both. Thereby philosophy proves that it can safely and happily survive its own death by keeping itself busy proving that it has actually died. Hume proved it. So did, on entirely different grounds, Hegel. So did the adherents of scientism, positivism, pragmatism, historicism; so did at least some of the existential thinkers; so did some mystics and some theologians. There is an immense variety of disconnected philosophical paths converging in one point of anti-philosophy. The farewell to philosophy never ends, like the 'bye-bye' in the famous sequence of a Laurel and Hardy film. What was once the kernel of philosophical reflection – being and non-being, good and evil, myself and the universe – seems to be repressed and reduced, except in the cause of historical enquiry, to almost such a dark corner in academia as God is in the departments of Divinity or as sexuality was in Victorian conversation.

7

What is repressed, banned from acceptable discourse and declared shameful is not done away with, however, if it makes up an unremovable part of culture. It either survives, temporarily silent, in the underground of civilization or seeks to find outlets in distorted expression. Victorian manners failed to abolish sex and God has not been buried forever in people's minds under the piles of books devoted to death-of-God theology and related exercises. Excommunications do not necessarily kill. The sensibility to traditional worries of philosophy has not withered away; it survives subcutaneously, as it were, ready to reveal its presence as a result of slight accidents.

That the sensibility survives does not entail that it consists of 'problems' to solve which a genius will one day come up with a reliable 'method'. If the word 'problem' suggests that a solving technique is in principle possible and may be found, the historical vicissitudes of philosophy can hardly fail to cast doubt on this hope; perhaps there are no 'problems' in this sense, just worries, and since the worries are real, it is reasonable to ask: where do they come from? How do we explain their presence? The same history which justifies strong doubt about their possible conversion into 'problems' provokes no less strong doubts about their eventual extinction. Philosophers who have abandoned the faith in universal norms of rationality – whether pragmatists or historicists – are in an awkward position: they live on those very worries which, they explain, we ought to get rid of altogether, as they make no sense and are of no imaginable practical use.

ITS SELF-YEARNING. JASPERS (1)

Another attitude is still available to us. We may admit that no traditional metaphysical questions are soluble and still deny that this is a reason to dismiss them or declare them meaningless. Philosophy, according to this view, is indeed the love of wisdom but this love is never consummated; any consummation is just an illusion, a poor satisfaction in the seeming certitude. If so, what might this futile search – known as such in advance – be for? The answer is: what matters is the search, for, however unsuccessful, it radically changes our lives. We ought to know that neither the empirically accessible universe nor the mathematical instruments we employ to describe it are self-explanatory and that the sought-after explanation will never be found, as to find it would require concepts and images which cannot be derived from this universe. Our language, no matter how it is stretched and twisted, is not capable of breaking out of its origin in the perception, imagination and logic which this universe has imposed on us. Briefly, we cannot pierce the mystery and convert it into knowledge, but to know that there is a mystery is important; although the veil will not be torn off from the ultimate reality, we ought to know that there is a veil. This is probably a fair summary of Jaspers' approach, even though he has not expressed it in so many words.

However, the same perennial sceptical argument can cast doubt on the consistency of such an approach. So conceived, philosophy is an exhortation to a hopeless quest for knowledge, rather than knowledge itself (a long exhortation, considering the overall volume of Jaspers' work). And yet, this exhortation is supposed to imply a knowledge about the limits of knowledge. We can never escape the infernal circle of epistemology: whatever we say, even negatively, about knowledge implies a knowledge we boast of having discovered; the saying 'I know that I know nothing', taken literally, *is* self-contradictory. Normal daily life and most of scientific communication between people do not require any epistemological premises, no presuppositions about truth in general or about relationships between perceptions and reality, and the most inveterate sceptic can well engage in verbal exchange with other people without interpreting it in philosophical terms. He can even use words like 'true' and 'false' in their current unreflective sense; but once he tries to explain why it is wrong to go beyond this usage and to look for the 'nature of truth', that is once he not only behaves like a sceptic but wants to justify his position, he is not consistent any longer.

Still, even without making such justifications, a sceptic is not necessarily blameless. If he forbears from talking about philosophy on the grounds that nothing can be said about it consistently and, besides, that the arguments which expose the nullity of philosophy presuppose, once uttered, impermissible philosophical premises, he simply refuses to give away a secret which he believes himself to be the keeper of. In other words, he admits to himself that he does possess a knowledge (about the impossibility of knowledge) to hand over which to other people would put him into a logically embarrassing position. Assuming that he has succeeded in purging his mind thoroughly, however, and thus that he no longer keeps in mind the grounds for his refusal, he is not a sceptic any longer; he must have simply forgotten that he had ever thought about philosophical issues or had been a sceptic. Is such a feat - deliberately and successfully to forget one's own past mental work, to clean out one's memory from logically undesirable ingredients and so to cheat oneself, so to speak - possible at all? Most probably not. Whatever the answer, a sceptic faces the dilemma: either he is not a sceptic at all in any sense, or his thinking is incoherent.

10

ITS SURVIVAL

But it seems that incoherence is unavoidable once genuinely philosophical questions are asked. The reason is simple: philosophy has been searching for an absolute language, a language which would be perfectly transparent and convey to us reality as it 'truly' is, without adulterating it in the process of naming and describing. This quest was hopeless from the start, for to phrase our questions we necessarily employ the contingent language as we find it ready-made and not concocted for metaphysical purposes. There is no absolute beginning in thinking, no absolute language (Plato knew that – witness *Cratylus*), and even no way how we could express in a contingent language – the only one at our disposal – the very concept of the absolute language (and thus the concept of the contingent language as well) or the absolute beginning. Inevitably, we start and end in the middle of our itinerary.

The awareness of this predicament is the sceptical Enlightenment, which includes awareness of the inconsistency which is as fatefully inherent in it as is circular reasoning or the *petitio principii* in the search for a 'presuppositionless' knowledge. It is arguable nonetheless that both this search and the sceptical demonstrations of its futility are, as it were, natural products of the very construction of human mind and cultural development; once philosophy appeared it was impossible to cancel it, no matter how often and how vociferously its nullity might have been denounced.

ON WHAT IS REAL

Why should we bother, indeed, about what is 'real' or 'unreal', 'true' or 'false', in other than a practically relevant sense? In daily life the former distinction is indispensable insofar as it contrasts dreams, illusions and hallucinations with other perceptions. This distinction has no metaphysical bearing. Dreams and illusions are events which happen and are obviously real in this sense. They are unreal to the extent they are not shared by other people and thus are not included in the communication process which has practical meaning. To be sure, dreams might be prophetic signs or God's announcements and thus acquire a social sense, but this does not abrogate the distinction between two kinds of perceptions; oneirology dwells in a communication system which is not translatable into the 'secular' one. We may either speak of two areas of reality, each of them governed by separate rules, or call one of them 'real' in contrast to the other – in either case the distinction is of no metaphysical character. I may dream about a fire in my house and then discover in my dream a hidden message from another world, but, once awake, I am not going to call firemen for help in fighting the disaster. In other words: 'real' and 'unreal' in the current sense are characteristics of the communication process and not of things themselves. Metaphysical search for what is 'really real', as opposed to what only appears to be, has not practical consequences (at least at first glance) and can be declared meaningless or dismissed on pragmatic grounds.

The same can be said about the 'true/false' distinction. In common usage it is clear enough and involves no metaphysical presuppositions about how the world 'really' is in contrast to how it appears to be. Again, nothing more seems to be needed for practical purposes; 'true' and 'false' are properties of the human communication process and they do not refer to the question of the correspondence between our judgements and reality 'in itself'.

We can only make guesses about the ultimate origin of the distinction between real and unreal in a sense which goes beyond the distinction between what is and what is not shared by people, and thus only speculate about the idea that perhaps the world we live in is an illusion or merely an appearance of a genuine reality, inaccessible to perception. This insight is, of course, older than philosophy (in the European sense of this word): we know it from Hindu and Buddhist wisdom.

One can certainly argue that this distinction was a necessary condition of the emergence of science in a modern sense (Whitehead made this point). It so happened that it was Democritus who said that 'in truth' there is nothing but atoms and void, but if nobody had come up with such a speculative idea, modern atomistic theory would never have arisen; it so happened that the Pythagoreans decided that numerical relationships had a sort of ontological priority over empirical phenomena, but someone had to assert the cognitive independence of mathematics from the experience if mathematics was to develop at all. Those arguments are probably sound, but they do not explain the origin of the distinction between appearance and reality; it might have been essential in the development of science, but incidentally so; mankind would not have been capable of building science had it not previously worked out the distinction between essence and phenomena (let us think of historians' insistence on Galileo's Platonism), but this distinction was not established in order to make science possible. Is there in the human mind a separate drive which compels us to suspect that the truly real world is hidden underneath the touchable surface? Do we carry a kind of distrustful instinct which, though often spurned and derided by sober empiricist reason, has never been entirely asleep throughout the history of civilization and which tries to persuade us that the divine eye (or transcendental ego) sees things quite differently from the way we do, and that we are not forever excluded from a share in this infallible vision?

The history of European metaphysics seems to be a desperately frustrating and ever attempted effort to express this instinct in a language which satisfies the requirements of Reason, which appointed itself with increasing self-assurance as the ultimate arbiter of validity. This self-appointment or self-anointment was in part spurious, in part genuine. It was spurious insofar as Reason defined itself by criteria which were taken up from the existing body of science and which therefore had no other validation than the sheer efficiency of science. It was genuine, however, to the extent it attacked metaphysics on logical grounds and implied that logic is an impassable pale beyond which no communication is possible and is, at least in this sense, an ultimate foundation.

Why, indeed, do so many philosophers devote their efforts to refuting the idea of solipsism and to proving that 'the world exists', given, firstly, that nobody has ever seen a deeply convinced and consistent solipsist and, secondly, that it seems to make not the slightest practical difference whether the world exists or not? Why should we be dissatisfied with the commonsense distinction between dreams and illusions on the one hand and the normal, that is, the universally shared, perceptions on the other and look instead for a method whereby we could convince ourselves that the universe we perceive is not a figment of imagination after all, but includes a sort of 'hard' reality? Why should there have been so many philosophers and mystics bold enough to work out the idea of 'Nothingness' and venture with dread into this imaginary abyss, instead of realising at the outset – as Carnap was to do in his famous attack on Heidegger – that 'Nothingness' is no more than a silly and illicit substantialization of the particle of negation, of the simple and most useful word 'not'?

Retrospectively – and speculatively, of course – we can understand why metaphysical questioning appeared, and even why it would have been strange if it had not. The source of our passionate search for 'reality' is our fragility which God or nature could not have prevented us from experiencing once he – or she, or they – had endowed us with the power to express in language both the distinction between illusion and non-illusion and the uncertainty of our life.

To be sure, there is such a well-known psychological phenomenon as a feeling – frequent but usually short lasting – or 'irreality' or 'de-realization', and it is even possible that it became the psychological background of Descartes' philosophy. But it is too volatile to explain the persistence of metaphysical quest. If indeed metaphysical feelings are neurotic symptoms, this must be, so to speak, an anthropologically grounded neurosis, a permanent, incurable – and potentially destructive – characteristic of a creature which, for better or worse, is capable of perceiving the precariousness of its individual and collective destiny, the unreliability of its endeavours and the fallibility of its knowledge.

If indeed metaphysics – that is the search for certainty and for the ultimate ground – is the expression of the experience of human fragility, if it is from this experience that comes the energy which ultimately keeps philosophy alive, this does not entail at all that metaphysical reflection is no more than an imaginary elixir invented to

15

appease a real discomfort. It is quite conceivable that the specifically human infirmity consisting in the awareness of being infirm, endows us with a peculiar sensitivity which opens our mind to new avenues of exploration and enables us to express the distinction between contingent and necessary, between what is acceptable and what is certain, between relative and absolute, between finite and infinite.

Descartes remarks (in his letter to Vatier on 22 February 1638) that the certainty of his proofs for God's existence depends on arguments which show the uncertainty of our knowledge of material things. Since Descartes dismissed – for reasons which do not need to occupy us now – the validity of Thomist arguments for God's existence and considered his own as the only reliable ones, it is clear that in his view we would have known nothing about God had we not realized how unreliable is everything we know about the universe, including its very existence. This remark is apparently an exception, a *hapax legomenon* in Descartes' work (he believed it improper to include it in a book which he wanted to be understandable even to women) and it is most revealing. It proves that he was aware of the fact that the only way to the Absolute Being is through the experience of the fragility of the world.

It needs stressing that to Descartes it is not only the fragility of the world which is an indispensable premise for our knowledge of the Absolute but my own fragility as well: not the uncertainty about my existence, of course, but the poverty of my cognitive powers; I know the perfect Being from the fact that I have its idea in my mind and my mind, being imperfect, would never have been capable of fabricating this idea from its own resources.

If we distil Descartes' intellectual effort to reach the absolute to this simple and general idea – we know the Absolute thanks to our awareness of the fragility of the world and of ourselves – we notice immediately that, thus reduced, this notion is applicable to nearly all attempts intellectually to tame the ultimate reality. All the five arguments of St Thomas Aquinas purport to show that the world, as we know it from experience, needs its cause and end; that its imperfection and non-self-sufficiency, if they are to be understood, require imperatively a perfect and necessary Being. Even the ontological argument, at least in the Cartesian version (in the response to the *Second Objection* to *Meditations*), refers directly to the distinction between the contingent and the necessary Being. Kant's practical reason postulates God as the highest good because the moral law provides no ground for a connection between morals and happiness; in other words, we have to accept God's necessary presence, according to Kant, because there is an empirically unbridgeable gap between our desire for happiness and the rational moral rules which bind us; if these two coincide, it is only by chance. To be sure, great neo-Platonists, from Plotinus and Proclus, through Maimonides and down to Spinoza, did not, at least not ostensibly, deduce the necessity of the Absolute from the contingency of the world, but every time we look more closely at the grounds of their belief, we discover the same insight: all the components of the empirically accessible universe, including ourselves, and the universe as a whole, are unintelligible by themselves – being corruptible, they cannot be self-rooted and they drift into an abyss, as it were, if no self-rooted reality is there to support them.

One may argue, in the Humean spirit, that this experience, when expressed in metaphysical parlance, is no

17

more than a tautology: once the assumption is made that everything needs a ground or a sufficient reason, then whatever is contingent must by definition be referred to something that is self-grounded; but the assumption is arbitrary.

Yet it is only an apparent tautology. It is true that once we speak of the 'contingent' or the 'relative' we evoke the 'necessary' and once we utter the deceptively obvious word 'finite' the seemingly unintelligible 'infinite' looms up automatically; to call the world 'contingent' – so the same argument goes – is indeed to postulate an Absolute Being, but the fallacy lies precisely in the use of non-empirical concepts both of which we may safely do without.

May we? This depends on what is the origin and the use of those concepts.

The sheer fact that each term of the pair 'contingent/necessary' or 'finite/infinite' is intelligible only as a term in a pair and cannot be defined without the help of its pendant, so that each supports the other, does not entail that they are empty or that expressions like 'the contingency of the world calls for an Absolute Being' are tautological. Concepts which are unquestionably rooted in experience display the same characteristic: they are understandable only in pairs of which the terms support each other ('big' and 'small', 'slow' and 'rapid', 'fluid' and 'solid' and so on). If all observable movements were of the same speed we could not have worked out the concepts of 'slow' and 'rapid' and if all bodies were of the same density the notions of 'fluid' and 'solid' would be unconstructible. The difference between these two kinds of concepts does not consist in that the latter are empirical whereas the former are not. The difference is historical and does not refer to supposedly immutable characteristics of experience. It is conceivable that the distinction between finite and infinite was first suggested by simple arithmetical and geometrical considerations (numbers, straight lines and the like). The distinction between contingent and necessary or between relative and absolute could not have emerged on mathematical grounds, however. It is founded on experience, not unlike the distinction between green and red, light and heavy, day and night. Why the former used to be dismissed as speculative, while the latter were accepted as sound, was because the distinction between, say, 'wet' and 'dry' is practically applicable, unlike the distinction between contingent and necessary. The difference is then pragmatic and is based on the implicit normative premise which restricts the idea of experience to that which is or might be useful in dealing with objects and is better or genuine in this sense. This premise is one of the intellectual founding blocks of modernity. It is ideological and justified by the utilitarian attitude to life, not by the perennial rules of rationality. This attitude, to which we owe our science and technology, requires standards whereby utilizable experience, the experience which is good for handling things, is to be defined and separated from the experience which could not be thus employed.

One might argue that metaphysical concepts have a place in the human life process, notably in the realm of religious worship. Yet, apart from the fact that in acts of worship 'practical application' means obviously something radically different – a knowledge involving such concepts cannot be converted into instruments of predicting or controlling natural phenomena – religious life is not built around the metaphysical qualities 'contingent' and 'necessary'. Personal gods whom people pray to, thank, obey, venerate or try to outwit, are by no means naturally identifiable with the absolute entity metaphysicians vainly attempted to domesticate in their idiom. Such identification did occur in European civilization as a result of extraordinary historical events but is not at all conceptually guaranteed. I shall presently revert to this question.

Retrospectively, it seems natural that the process which resulted in separating empirical (in the sense of efficiently applicable) distinctions from metaphysical ones had to take the sceptical, and then idealistic, form. In its crucial phase, in late medieval nominalism, basic Cartesian and Humean insights were already worked out: apart from the principle of contradiction, the only certainty I can gain in natural knowledge, both John of Mirecourt and Nicholas of Autrecourt argued, is my own existence (*quod de substantia materiali alia ab anima nostra non habemus certitudinem evidentiae*, claims one of the sixty erroneous statements of Nicholas, condemned in 1347); the reality of substance is as little provable as are natural causal relationships, and people would be much better off if, instead of perusing Aristotle's treatises, they concentrated on learning what little can be effectively learnt. Since God, being omnipotent, can produce appearances which we are incapable of distinguishing from real things, there is simply no point in investigating what is real in the world of sense-experience as opposed to what merely seems to be. Peter d'Ailly made a similar point later on. There may be no direct proof of continuity from the fourteenth- and fifteenth-century Cartesians and Humeans to the great and famous thinkers who were to inflict the last *coup de grâce* on the metaphysics of old three or four centuries later. But nobody doubts that modern empiricism and scepticism emerged from the soil which was fertilized by those early bold attempts on the entire conceptual apparatus of the Schools.

The attacks on the Aristotelian heritage left the distinction between dreams and reality intact. Their point was to cancel the distinction - empirically unfeasible - between reality and irreality in a metaphysical sense. Without necessarily saying so in so many words, they made the very concept of existence useless, unless it was applicable to two ultimate realities: God and myself.

And here the *horror metaphysicus* sets in. Let us unwind it.

CARTESIAN DREAMS. RECYCLING THE *COGITO*

The horror consists in this: if nothing truly exists except for the Absolute, the Absolute is nothing; if nothing truly exists but myself, I am nothing.

Let us look at this dizzy drift into nothingness first from the Cartesian end.

Descartes' *opinio somnii*, dream-argument, might appear, in the *Meditations*, no more than a logical device which, on a circuitous route, leads us to the restoration of the reality of the world. Yet it has emerged from the alarming experience which caught him and which happens to many people: perhaps I am dreaming right now? Perhaps everything I perceive is just an illusion?

It has been pointed out by many critics that, in order to ask the question, Descartes must have already known the difference between a dream and the waking state and therefore he could not have consistently imagined that there is nothing in his environment but dreamy figments of his mind. Against this objection some of his defenders reply that Descartes did not imagine he may have been dreaming all the time; his point was only that in no particular moment could he be certain that he was *not* dreaming.

Yet Descartes' question clearly aims at the entire physical universe. The whole content of experience was in the shadow of doubt. Perhaps it is inconsistent to ask a question which envisages the possibility that I am dreaming incessantly, if 'dreaming' is defined by contrast to the waking state. Dreaming does not need to be so conceived, however; Descartes argued that all waking perceptions might conceivably be similar to a dream in a sense that there was nothing in 'reality' which corresponded to them. I have no guarantee against the suspicion that God or a malicious demon, for reasons known to them only, feeds me with illusory pictures of a world that 'does not exist'.

A radical empiricist's reply to this terror of illusion is that it does not matter at all whether or not the world exists and that indeed this very distinction is meaningless and inexpressible; since the assumption that the world 'does not exist' makes no change in my experience and since, by definition, all distinctions concerning 'the state of the world' have a meaning only insofar as they can be described in empirical terms, there is simply no empirical difference – and thus no difference at all – between a world which exists and a world which does not – not only for all practical purposes but for purely theoretical investigations those worlds are identical. A radical empiricist (like Mach) cancels the Cartesian question by invalidating the (unutterable) contrast between two universes which consist of mental and physical events respectively. The very notions of existence and reality (unless they are empirically definable, as in the distinction between hallucinations and normal perceptions) became useless and misleading.

Is there anything wrong with this simple solution? Why are we naturally reluctant to be satisfied with it? Do we need the concept of reality and of existence in a metaphysical sense? I shall argue that we do and that therefore the *Cogito* can be partially vindicated: not that the act of *Cogito* provides us with an unshakeable foundation of knowledge or an ultimate source of certainty, but in the sense that it might provide us with a paradigm of the notion of existence.

The discussion can be aided by a mental experiment. Let us suppose that – as some super-experts on the afterlife teach us – we will be able to produce in heaven instantaneously, by a sheer act of will, any physical environment; a simple fiat will build around us the Himalayas, Paris, an Amazonian forest, or the lunar desert. Such worlds, thus mentally fabricated, would be 'unreal' in the sense Descartes tried to elucidate, but they would not differ at all from our perceptions of the 'real' ones. Would the awareness of their irreality bother us at all? Perhaps not, perhaps we would enjoy mountains, rivers, cities and forests as much as we do now and we would neither feel that there was something wrong with their illusory status, nor be properly able to describe how illusions differ from non-illusions. But what about other people? It is easy to see that this would make an enormous difference. If we were aware that all the people we communicate with in the celestial abode, our friends and loved ones, are artificial figments created at will by our mental acts and have no subjective life of their own, we would be extremely worried, our perception of life would be entirely changed and we would be overwhelmed by a feeling of unbearable solitude. The same would occur, of course, if we seriously gave credence to another Cartesian suggestion: that other people we meet in the terrestial life are perhaps nothing but automata, having no mental life, no lived experience of their own, and we find ourselves alone in the company of such artificial beings, undistinguishable from real people but mechanically manufactured, as they often appear in science fiction.

And so, we go back to the eternal problem of the reality of subjectivity, which, no matter how often it might have been exorcized, has haunted European philosophy for over three centuries. The basic data of the problem are quite simple. Granted that subjectivity, i.e. the quality of an experience consisting in that it is mine, cannot be handed over or, rather, shown to other people, it is, on the empiricist assumption, irrelevant to our lives and all its derivates can easily be eliminated from our discourse. The assumption is that only those sides of experience which can be shared with other people are 'real', and the subjective side cannot be converted into a common good. The discussions on 'thinking machines' boil down to the validity of this assumption which establishes a standard whereby reality or irreality is to be measured. What can compel us to accept this assumption? Nothing. It is arbitrary and it expresses a historically shaped hierarchy of goods (cognitive validity is ultimately defined by pragmatic values).

The mental experiment just described also suggests that the word 'existence' refers to two kinds of intuition. In both daily life and scientific discourse the 'existence' of objects can be safely relegated to the human communication process. It is an aspect of this process and in this sense it is relative, whether the objects under scrutiny are commonly accepted as 'real' (like mountains, magnetic fields and quarks) or their reality is contestable, uncertain or doubtful (like tachyons, angels, numbers and values). Real is what is real within the historically established rules of human communication. This pink elephant I am just seeing in the corner of my room is unreal in the sense that I am alone to perceive it and no-one else shares my vision which can for this reason be dismissed as a result, say, of my alcoholic delirium. Mountains and quarks are real by the same rules of reference. By the same rules the reality of tachyons, angels and numbers is possible yet uncertain. We do not need more for the practical purposes which the communication process aims at; we can do without 'existence' in the metaphysical sense, i.e., the presence of self-referring entities of which the properties are there irrespective of whether or not they are perceived, named and identified in our communication. Since by definition we are not capable of determining, by means independent of our perception and language, to what extent our perception and language contribute to the picture of the world we perceive and talk about (apart from individual distortions, like in the case of the pink elephant) the abstractly concocted doctrine of collective solipsism – in a neo-Kantian, historicist or pragmatic version – is irrefutable. That the reality of objects is relative to a linguistic game, to universal patterns of perception and to practical needs which shape our way of organising the world, cannot be disproved without a vicious circle. To be sure, the self-reference paradox, already mentioned, will not cease tormenting us but we can avoid it in the radically sceptical fashion, stop articulating our multi-solipsism, stop bothering about metaphysics and declare the matter of 'existence' an insoluble or meaningless or – better – inexpressible question

It is not so, however, with the intuition of existence once I deal with the self-referring identity that is myself. The Cartesian separation of this privileged reality from the reality of everything else conforms to a most basic and unphilosophical insight. I cannot say with conviction 'I am a part of a linguistic game', 'my reality is relative to historically established patterns of perception', 'that I exist means that it is useful to believe I do', 'I do not exist etc. That I am is indeed irrefutable and to this extent the 'existence' in a metaphysical, non-relative sense becomes intelligible to me.

But, if it is irrefutable (in the sense that nobody can either argue against it or declare it unintelligible), is it not just trivially true? And why does it matter? There is no other answer than this: it matters not because it might provide a basis for a construction of an epistemology, let along of science, as Descartes would have it, but because it supplies us with the only direct intuition of existence. Nothing else can be deduced from the *Cogito*. And if indeed we admit that the *Cogito* is a paradigmatic case which makes existence intelligible, it is not applicable to non-subjective reality. It is not paradigmatic, after all.

And why does it matter at all that we have the intuition of existence? It does not matter – or so it seems – for any practical purposes. The easiest answer to the question 'why does it matter?' is simply: because many people feel it does; the cognate questions like 'why is it interesting?', 'why is it important?', are in the same position. We may ask further: 'why do people feel it matters?' 'Why should we wish that what we accept is not only acceptable according to pragmatic criteria – not necessarily pragmatic in terms of a momentary usefulness or of an individual profit, but in terms of long-term social benefits (whatever that means) – but *true* in a metaphysical sense as well?'

ALIBI. THE CURSE OF TIME

Nietzsche's answer was that this desire for truth above utility is no more than one of many symptoms of human weakness, of our inability to rely on ourselves, to carry the burden of our solitude, to assert our will as the ultimate ground of everything we believe and to realize that we are self-grounded and not protected by any universal order of things.

Perhaps. Assuming that he was right, however, it does not follow that we are wrong in realizing our weakness; the feeling of weakness may be, after all, not only causally explicable but well-justified in terms of the very order of things which Nietzsche dismissed, praising (as well as being frightened by) the eternal chaos out of which the self-rooted invincible will should emerge, and empty will void of content. He was not consistent on this point, though, as with most other areas of his philosophizing: he glorified the spirit of doubt, but if there is no such thing as truth, there cannot be doubt either. My act of doubting implies that I believe something to be true, but I am unable to decide what is. Once the quality 'true' is abrogated, doubting is pointless.

And from the fact that we need an order, it does not follow that there is none, even if Nietzsche is right in pointing out that arguments for the beliefs which conform to our wishes ought to be *prima facie* treated with suspicion. We may need an order and wish it to be real but it still may be real, not just a concoction of our wishful thinking.

That the need to live in an ordered world, a world of which the origin, rules and destiny we can grasp, is not a temporary, historically relative whim, but a lasting part of our constitution as humans, the entire history of religion

- a perennial aspect of culture - is there to demonstrate. In pointing out that this need arises out of a feeling of weakness, Nietzsche was perfectly in agreement with Christian tradition and probably with religious tradition *tout court*. The crucial insight we find in religious experience, repeatedly recurring in various sacred books, may be summed up in one single word: alibi - elsewhere.

That we are elsewhere implies, throughout the history of religion, that there is a home where we belong, that we live in exile; to be elsewhere is a permanent human condition on earth. Neo-Platonic philosophy identified the 'elsewhere' as time, and Plotinus provided subsequent centuries with an insight which, in various versions, kept surfacing in philosophy up to, and including, our century (Bergson, Husserl, Heidegger, Sartre). The very fact that we are, in every moment, in the 'moving' present (as opposed to the divine eternal present), losing forever the moment just passed, amounts to saying that we can never be sure what it is 'to be', because the direct experience is not of being, but of unceasingly losing our existence in the irretrievable 'has been'. Since the present, on closer inspection - as St Augustine argued - shrinks to nothing, and since the physical universe, having no awareness of time, has no part in time either (i.e. no memory and thus no past), but its time is ours, this experience leads to an alarming suspicion that such an evasive and slippery idea as 'to be' is simply beyond our grasp. This might be a cause for despair if there were no Absolute Being which can restore our assurance and the feeling that there is an order after all.

Sartre would not have been pleased if he had been told that he was an incomplete disciple of St Augustine. But what he took over from Heidegger was deeply rooted in the history of ancient and medieval metaphysics with which he was probably not well acquainted. To say that a human self-referring existence is never self-identical or that it is not what it is because of its time-bound nature, is an ancient insight; both in pagan neo-Platonist and in Christian medieval thought it seemed to imply logically a self-identical, timeless entity – the One – lest we were compelled to admit the depressingly nonsensical conclusion that 'nothing is.' Sartre, of course, refused to play with fire (i.e. with the idea of the Absolute in the Platonic sense); he was satisfied with defining human existence as a pure negation and the non-human reality as an ever impenetrable, self-contained and indifferent entity of whose mode of being we know nothing. It was not supposed to be a higher or the highest, or the most sublime form of spirit, but rather inertness itself and thus something that would, perhaps not improperly, be called 'nothing'. Are we dealing with two kinds of nothingness facing each other in radical inability to communicate, both definable only negatively, as the opposite of the other term? Sartre seems to neglect the simple fact that our bodies are a part of this inert Being-in-itself; indeed the fact that we have bodies appears to be an inconvenient and an embarrassing obstacle which disturbs clarity of thought. To get rid of this fact would make us better off in terms of philosophical Cartesian consistency.

THE ABSOLUTE (1)

From the fragments of Parmenides which remain we cannot guess how he arrived at his concept of the Being but, when we look at the vicissitudes of his insight in pagan Greek and then Christian thought, we cannot resist feeling that there has been a kind of mental compulsion which stood behind the quest for the *Ultimum* or rather two *Ultima* which are not necessarily identical. What is looked for is, firstly, the cause or the creator of the visible universe, and, secondly, the self-supporting, self-grounding, logically necessary ground of whatever exists contingently. The first *Ultimum* explains the actual origin of the world, the second makes the world possible at all; the former provides us with the answers to the question 'where do stars, earth, planets and human creatures come from?'; the latter lets us understand how anything finite and corruptible can exist at all or, 'if everything is finite and corruptible, how is it possible that everything has not been converted into nothing?'. The first *Ultimum* is open to people in religious myths. The second was elaborated in philosophical enquiry once it separated itself from mythology; so it was at any rate in European civilization, whereas both in the Vedic and Buddhist traditions metaphysical insight and religious myth seem to have emerged jointly.

The philosophical search for the *Ultimum* as it developed in neo-Platonist thought revealed the same intellectual drive that was to show itself subsequently in the ontological argument for God's existence, and in the argument from the contingency of the world. We may sum up this drive in a single intuition: if the world is more than a self-annihilating abyss, there must be something that is bound to exist, or of which non-existence would be both a logical and ontic self-contradiction. This last distinction is indispensable. What is meant by saying that the *Ultimum*'s (or the Absolute's) existence is necessary is not only that we, humans, are incapable of conceiving its absence within our usual logical rules of thinking, as it cannot be a priori certaint that our logic is infallible. We may find those rules irresistibly binding, but we are finite and contingent creatures and our logic might be no less contingent, and from the fact that we do not have the choice *not* to obey it, it does not follow that the ultimate reality has to obey it as well. What is thus meant by the necessity of the *Ultimum*'s existence is that this necessity is its own and not ours. Our logic discovers the self-contradiction in the Absolute's non-existence because its non-self-contradiction is actually there, and not vice versa. Of course, we cannot discover this self-contradiction without first relying upon our logical norms which then are supposed to derive their validity from the source of being; the never-ending curse of the vicious circle does not cease operating here, as in any search for the ultimate foundation. But the vicious circle is a natural result of the simple fact that we are not gods, that is to say, we can never – apart perhaps from through mystical experience – start our search from the epistemological zero-point, without presuppositions.

It is natural to ask: if this diabolical circle is inescapable in all our attempts to reach the absolute within our logical discourse, why should not we simply declare that this search is no more than a wanton hunting for chimera and halt it, as a matter of common sense? Many philosophers have asked precisely that, and answered by saying that it is much better, indeed, to abandon this Sysyphian effort. This does not prevent others from trying. It seems that quite simply – all the pronouncements of empiricists, pragmatists and sceptics about the imminent, final and world-wide triumph of their approach notwithstanding – the search for the ultimate foundation is as much an unre-movable part of human culture as is the denial of the legitimacy of this search. The denial, once articulated in philosophical idiom – and not simply practised by giving up the very act of questioning – is, as I have argued, no less arbitrary than what it denies; any explanation of the denial involves logical and empirical rules of which the validity is open to question. The point is not merely that the most arduous and arid metaphysical investigations are not vain as they might have a real, though often strange and unpredictable, impact on the course of world affairs and affect, through convoluted routes, human life (without Proclus there would have been no Hegel, and without Hegel today's world would not be what it is). The point is rather than it is impracticable to eradicate from the human mind the desire of truth in the common sense of this word, the simple and elementary desire to know what is 'truly true', true without qualifications, true quite apart from our thinking and perceiving, from our practical considerations and from usefulness. This desire is unlikely to be a derivate of the normal and obvious need to distinguish illusions from valid perceptions or mistakes from correct reasoning. That something seems to be true and turns out not to be is a daily occurrence and to employ this distinction we do not need the idea of 'truth' in the just cited metaphysical sense. But our minds want to know what is true even if it does not seem to matter at all, simply to know how the world actually is, and this need obviously coincides with the idea of reality which is there irrespective of its being known and perceived Once we know that errors and illusions occur, questions about a reality which can never be an illusion, or the truth about which no mistakes are possible, are unavoidable. In vain do we condemn this desire as a perversion of a good and easily understandable quest for a more frugal 'truth', for a truth which we have to take into account in practical matters and which is a part of our communal life. To shrug off the issue and to ask 'why should we bother?' is easy and unproductive.

THE ABSOLUTE (2)

Once the quest for Truth and Reality – spelt with capital letters – is accepted as a structural part of culture or of human minds, it is easy to see that it cannot be satisfied with anything less than the Absolute. No particular truth – either empirical or mathematical – that is to say, no truth within our reach, can be perfectly certain and unassailable for ever unless it can be seen as a part of the whole truth. Firstly, this is because we can never be sure how the whole truth might alter the meaning of a particular truth or limit the scope of its validity. Secondly, it is because we never arrive at the knowledge of any particular truth without using some presuppositions or rules which guide our reasoning or the way we express our experience, and those rules and presuppositions, unquestionable though they might appear, are not self-grounded; one may always ask about the reasons for them and this process of asking is infinite. Any particular truth could consequently be converted into Truth only on the condition that it coincides with a particular truth which is a part of or an aspect of the whole Truth, i.e. only if it is seen as truth by the infallible eye of the all-knowing subject. This subject, in order to meet the requirement of omniscience or to be the repository of Truth in the unrestricted sense, has to be everything it knows and to be perfectly self-transparent, as any distance between it and what it knows would abolish the certainty and the Wholeness. And if there is no Truth in this sense, there are no criteria whereby the real could be told from the unreal, indeed the very distinction is inexpressible; whatever is contingently real, is real on the condition that something else is real non-contingently, that is to say, is self-grounded. This is the explicit or implicit foundation of neo-Platonism.

This entails that any particular true sentence refers to the whole of truth and truth is the referent of a true sentence, as some Platonizing logicians (like Lukasiewicz) accept.

Once we arrive at self-grounding reality, identical with Truth, the same Platonist logic leads inescapably to its other characteristics.

It is infinite (qualitatively, as the Germans like to say). That is to say, it cannot be limited, let alone destroyed, and thus cannot be affected by anything that is not itself. To enjoy logically necessary, self-supporting existence amounts, indeed, to being utterly impassible; an entity which is subject to changes or alterations caused by anything else would be corruptible and destructible, which is obviously incompatible with being 'infinite' (i.e. perfectly autonomous) and uncaused.

Consequently there is only one. This at least is self-evident in Platonic thinking, as if there were more than one Absolute, they would limit each other and none would meet the requirement of infinity. This conclusion, at first glance, might be questioned on the following ground: if 'infinity' means perfect self-containment or self-closedness, the inability to be affected by anything else, there is no reason why indefinitely many Absolutes could not co-exist in total mutual indifference, each of them neither knowing anything of the others nor being perturbed by their presence. Criticisms along such lines would be invalid, of course, if the infinitude were to equal omnipotence and thus be converted into 'quantitative' infinitude, as more than one almighty entity is inconceivable. The Platonists did not necessarily mention omnipotence as such, but they all implied that a real and intelligible – albeit indirect – relationship does obtain between the Absolute and the universe of finite minds and bodies as we know it. This assumption, though weaker than that of omnipotence, is nonetheless sufficient to counter the hypothesis of more than one Absolute; if the universe is dependent – whatever that means – on the Absolute, the Absolute is indeed bound to be unique, otherwise two or more Absolutes would limit, or compete with, each other, thus invalidating the assumption of self-sufficiency.

We have touched the point which has always been crucial in speculation about the supreme, self-rooted Reality: may we assume that the finite reality depends on it, and if so, in what sense? If not, how could the supreme Reality be known to us at all and why should it be one only? If so, does it remain, within the reach of our conceptual capacity, the *Ultimum* we want it to be?

The Absolute, according to the same Platonic dialectic, is pure actuality, that is to say, it does not allow distinctions between what it can be and what it is; it is everything it can be. This seems to follow, again, from the very concept of a being which is bound to exist by virtue of its nature: it is immutable because necessarily to be is to be 'perfect' in the sense of 'completed'. It is inconceivable that something could be added to, or taken away from, a being which is incapable of being created; it can as little be improved or degraded as a mathematical theorem.

Therefore the Absolute is timeless and not everlasting. If it could remember the past as past, i.e. as something that was but is not any longer, and anticipate the future as such, i.e. as what is not yet but is going to be, and if it had to arrive at self-understanding by the intermediary of memory and anticipation, it would never be complete, never whole, but always compelled to distinguish in itself between what it is and what it could be. Again, it is as timeless as a mathematical equation.

It is now easy to notice that one expression in the above description needs to be corrected. The saying that the Absolute is impassible and 'cannot be affected by anything that is not itself' is wrong if it implies that it can, indeed, be affected by itself. It cannot, though, as this would make it susceptible to change, too, and thus incomplete or imperfect. It is perfectly simple; were it not, were it composed of parts, had it separable qualities, it would not be necessarily immutable; some of its qualities (for instance intellect and will in a divine being: a paradigmatic example in scholastic theology) or parts would interfere with, or influence, each other, or operate separately, thus abrogating the completeness. The Absolute is as simple as a geometrical point.

All the characteristics listed above and familiar to all students of neo-Platonic tradition and medieval theology – self-sufficiency, impassibility, infinity, uniqueness, pure actuality, timelessness, simplicity – seem to imply each other; that is to say none of them may be asserted severally.

DIVINE PERSONS AND UNPERSONS.
IS GOD GOOD? *CRUOR DEI*

Once we know all that and know in addition that all these qualities have been attributed to God by the mainstream of Christian theology, we are immediately caught in a horrifying metaphysical snare. How can the *Ultimum*, thus identified, be the creator whose fiat called the universe into existence and how may goodness, love or benevolence in any recognizable sense be attributed to it? How could it be a *person?*

Readers of Plotinus know that his One retains some faint traces of personal life. While nameless (*Enn.*, V. 3.13; VI. 9.5) and nameless to such an extent that even the words 'One' (V. 4.1) and 'is' (VI. 8.8) are not properly applicable to it, the self-sufficient One is goodness itself (II. 9.1); it is love (VI. 8.15) and it is the natural place to which we want to return (VI. 9.9), however dimly we may perceive our own desire; it is our ultimate protection or even our own nature, screened from us by our contact with matter, i.e. evil.

Proclus identified the One with the Good, to be sure, but the readers of his *Elements of Theology* are at a loss in trying to guess what this Goodness is supposed to be. To him it is a matter of axiomatic self-evidence that whatever is differentiated, or consisting of parts, is secondary to the One; which suggests that the reality of the One is conceptually assured by the very presence of variety. Later on he explains that the Good is the first cause the reality of which is proved by the fact that things have to have causes and the series of causes cannot be infinite. Why the first cause should be good is not explained, however, and certainly it cannot be explained, as the Good, being axiomatically co-extensive with the Being (or 'transcendental' in the mediaeval sense of this word) appears a non-relative quality.

This peculiar neo-Platonic concept of goodness, once taken over by scholastic teaching, was applied to the God-person, thus burdening our minds with more mysteries. God, according to this teaching, is good in the sense of benevolent and caring about his creatures, but this is not the *reason* why his is good. The goodness we witness is only an expression of his intrinsic goodness which is not defined by his attitude to us; in other words, God would be perfectly and immutably good even if he had remained an otiose Absolute, producing nothing. This seems to violate our linguistic habits which imply that 'good' is a relative characteristic and involves, to make sense, an intention directed towards something or someone else. Goodness that is self-centred, non-intentional and yet actual, not potential, seems to be beyond our conceptual resources. To reply that God's benevolence towards us (assuming that it is empirically and irresistibly demonstrated, which some people doubt) expresses his intrinsic goodness and therefore provides us with a proof that he is good in himself, is to beg the question. From God's benevolence, as displayed in his works, we can infer nothing about his intrinsic goodness, as distinct from those works; otherwise we should suppose that in himself he is only potentially good, which would run counter to his perfect actuality. From 'transcendental' to revealed goodness there is no conceptually legitimate transition; the former, if it is known, can only be known a priori and it is indefinable in terms of actual benevolence. The gap between the One which is inherently good and the divine protector who is good to us, remains unbridgeable. Briefly, goodness, conceived of as an inherent property of the Absolute being, does not explain this Being's benevolence.

Yet this may not be the end of the story. We must never assume that great philosophers simply spin their web of abstractions for its own sake, and that there are no important reasons – albeit not always clearly understood by the philosophers themselves – behind their most abstruse constructions. Perusing Plato's *Parmenides* or Proclus' *Elements* (or Hegel's *Phenomenology*, for that matter) might drive one into despair. Is the former (apart from possibly being the self-refutation of the theory of ideas) just an exercise in dizzy dialectics of concepts, bearing no relation to our lives (or even a joke, as some believed)? Is the latter an incoherent and indigestible mass of empty abstractions, from which no path leads to people's common and universally experienced worries? I do not think so. Even if we assume that everything that matters in philosophy has been said by the Greeks and humbly accept, without being upset, our position of epigons, there is still a never-ending job of converting old insights into an idiom which might be intelligible today to our fellow men, and this is perhaps enough.

The idea of intrinsic goodness, not unlike many other crucial concepts in philosophy, may be made intelligible by its hypothetical mythological origin.

The gods in various mythologies are not necessarily good either in the sense of being kind and helpful to people or that of providing us with models of moral conduct; some are, some are not, and many display both good and evil sides in their adventures. But good in mythologies seems to be invariably linked with peace and harmony, evil with war, chaos and destruction. Once the myths are sublimated into metaphysical speculation, these elementary insights naturally tend to achieve a complete conceptual consistency: if good equals peace and harmony, perfect good equals perfect peace and harmony, and this means the perfect absence of tension, and thus, ultimately, absolute undifferentiation and immobility, or One. The more unity, the more goodness – this is Proclus' and the Platonists' unquestionable axiom. And so, when the good reaches the point of completeness, it loses any recognizable quality of goodness; by achieving perfection, the goodness vanishes. Since the One remains impassible in its total unity, it seems to be severed from any reality other than itself. Life, at least in the sense we are able to conceive, involves differentiation and tension; one reaches a complete peace by reaching lifelessness.

Therefore, the Absolute that was supposed to explain the very act of existence, is reduced, as a result of its own perfection, to non-existence and sinks into irrelevance. By being supremely real, it converts into unreality.

The most distressing problem of neo-Platonism consists in its incapacity to explain how the One could be creative and responsible for the visible universe. No matter how numerous might be the intermediary stages or emanations, spanning the space between its unspeakable unity and the miserable world we dwell in, the first step from the Absolute down to anything less-than-Absolute is bound to remain mysterious or simply impossible.

Proclus' One or the Good is called both *arche* and the first cause of everything. By being the Good itself, it is superior to self-sufficient entities which are just (adjectively) good. The hierarchy of being is defined by relationships of dependence or participation: the lower degrees partake in the higher; and yet the ultimate reality, the One, is incapable of being participated in, i.e. nothing can partake in it. What the actual succession of the degrees of being is, is not unambiguously clear, but this does not matter much when we wrestle with the riddle of the Eschaton. It appears that what comes after the first principle are gods or divine *henads*, then the Being, then Life and then *Nous* or Mind out of which the cosmos has emerged. Gods let lower principles partake in their goodness yet nothing can partake in the First. And Proclus does not seem able to say how the First can then be the first cause. We are taught that all things tend towards the Good and eventually reach it, having proceeded through all the intermediary rungs of the ontic ladder and thus completing the eternal and eternally moving circle of creation: from the first cause to the lowest souls back to the first cause. And yet nothing in this proto-Hegelian cycle can fill the conceptual breach between the First and the rest: not only because the self-contained First cannot have reason to go out of itself, but because this appears to be ontologically impossible, for all creatures, by definition, take something from, or participate in, or are given something by, the Creator and this is precisely what the very status of the One makes unfeasible. Moreover Proclus avers – quite consistently – that while the divine things, inaccessible to our reason, may nevertheless be known through inferior, dependent entities, the single First is totally unknowable. If so, we have to presume that to call it the first cause and to make the cosmos its – however remote – outflow is not only impermissible, but outright wrong. The circle which has neither a beginning nor an end – *kuklon anarchon kai ateleuteton* – cannot include, without self-contradiction, the unconditioned ground. Even to call it the First, let alone the first cause, is probably to abuse the language, granted that there is no meaning of 'First' without 'Second' being presupposed, and the One presupposes nothing.

The hierarchical order of things, from the One to matter, is not to be conceived in Platonic terms as a temporal succession; neither is it a series of purely logical relationships in the sense we usually mean when speaking of deductive reasoning. It is rather a 'phenomenological' (in the Hegelian sense) succession which may perhaps be called a causality without time and without the exchange of energy. And yet, even with this restriction, it is incomprehensible how the perfectly isolated One could be a cause of anything, considering that it is immutably undifferentiated and its goodness is no more than another name of its unity, and this name is known a priori. If unity is a necessary characteristic of a reality which is incapable of being created, it rather appears that to be incapable of being created is to be incapable of creating as well. Is God, so conceived, fatefully infertile?

Our meagre conceptual tools might again perhaps be aided by mythological imagery. In many archaic cosmological myths the universe emerges out of a primordial god who is torn apart, a god-martyr who sacrifices himself in the act of creation. This divine self-immolation explains the origin of cosmos but at the price of the creator's immutability. Cosmos becomes *cruor Dei*, God's blood, a result of his infinite self-inflicted suffering.

This frequent topic of archaic cosmogonies in various civilizations seems, of course, utterly incompatible with any religion of one God-creator. Do we not hear, however, an echo of the same myth in the Christian image of the divine Logos who recreates the world and restores its pristine innocence by a voluntary self-sacrifice? Does not the theology of the cross and redemption reassert this deeply-rooted mythological insight that a real creator has to be a *suffering God* and thus a God who denies his own God-head, as Jesus Christ denied it by assuming a life in flesh?

Some heretical or semi-heretical trends in Christian thought went further in trying to assimilate the myth of the bleeding God, in order to cope with the incongruity which theology inescapably faced once the biblical God had merged with Proclus' first principle. Meister Eckhart's God, self-projecting himself into the world and so becoming 'something', wounds himself, so to speak, so that he could be born in human soul.

DAMASCIUS AND TWO KINDS OF NOTHINGNESS

There are two great neo-Platonists who tried to go as far as possible in robbing the One of all human-like or person-like qualities and to preserve, nonetheless, the idea of creation: Damascius and Spinoza.

Damascius, the last head of the Academy until it was closed by the Emperor Justinian in 529, is still *merum nomen* even among philosophers, apart from those who devote special attention to neo-Platonic thought. This author of the last major work of pagan philosophy in Europe offered us perhaps the final, consummate product of a millennium of speculations on the ultimate ground (a full millennium, indeed, considering that Parmenides' acme, it is usually assumed, fell on about 475 BC). His *Problems and Solutions* (or *On Principles*), an enormously long and desparately chaotic work is, if possible, even more consistent than Proclus' *Elements* in avoiding any contact with any reality, whether physical or mental, which we might have an intuitive access to. Damascius' mind seems to abhor not only the body, like Plotinus, but life as well, and to move in the heaven of pure 'onta', stripped of anything except the very act of being.

Damascius accepts as a matter of course the perennial Platonic dogma: the fact that there are many things and not one requires an explanation which is necessarily given by something that includes no plurality, that is One; that the manifold cannot be a primordial fact, that the One is real, indeed that it is supremely and uniquely real, seems almost tautologically true in neo-Platonic thinking.

And yet, the One is not the *Ultimum*, not the last and the highest. As Parmenides' Being was to Plotinus a secondary level beyond which the unspeakable One vaults the entire hierarchy of reality, so in Damascius' speculation the One or the first cause becomes itself secondary and is located below the nameless darkness which no concept, no thought, no intuition could ever reach.

This quest for higher and higher levels of being may be accounted for by the very nature of language, once this dogma has been established. Whatever we say, even negatively, about the first principle, we naturally imply that something can be said about it and that it is not absolutely ineffable, after all, and this prompts us to look for a principle beyond the First, and this newly-discovered principle would be so ineffable that even to call it ineffable would be wrong. The search never ends, alas. To say that it is even improper to attribute ineffability to the *Ultimum* amounts to labelling it with another predicate; 'being so ineffable as not to be capable of being called ineffable' is no less a predicate than 'being ineffable'. One cannot speak with silence; it is as simple as that. By saying that a reality is utterly ineffable or utterly unknowable we fall fatally into the self-reference antinomy. Damascius knew that (as St Augustine did before him, for that matter), but found no solution except for describing the *Ultimum* by double denial (ineffability beyond ineffability), thus recreating the same antinomy. If after Damascius there had been a philosopher who continued the same line of reasoning, he would probably have tried to climb to a still higher level of reality in order to avoid the paradox - theoretically this process could go on indefinitely.

In fact Damascius, while looking for what would be higher than the highest, doubles the same incoherence:

the procession of things from the One is as little understandable as that of One from the absolutely ineffable.
The One is by definition perfectly simple, has no relationships to anything else or, for that matter, to itself (*On
Principles*, 13). It is unknowable, it knows neither anything beyond itself (higher or lower) nor itself (26), but
the fact that it cannot be known can be known (6); it is
the first cause of everything, which suggests that it needs
its metaphysical offspring. Indeed, Damascius notices the
contradiction while clumsily trying to explain it away: the
One as such needs nothing, not even itself (having no self-
relations), in order to be what it is; as the creative first
principle, however, it does need something else (13).
Damascius thus reveals the perplexing and probably
incurable inconsistency in the very concept of the creative
Absolute. The creative God of Christian tradition is love
and we easily associate love with procreation, but we are
never sure how love, which implies a need of someone
other than oneself, is to be reconciled with the perfect self-
closedness and self-sufficiency of the Absolute Being. Yet
there is no mention of love or of benevolence in the case
of Damascius' One: it seems to be a pure act of being One
and nothing else. There is no more than a hint of mystical
henosis in Damascius: the One, albeit not absolutely
ineffable, cannot be expressed by words, not even
negatively; it cannot be positioned or located (which
apparently means that there is no way of defining it with
the aid of other concepts) and what our mind reaches
when it approaches the One is not knowledge any longer,
but union (49). This sounds very Platonic, no doubt. But
Damascius does not try to explain this union. Nor is there
any suggestion to the effect that what he has in mind is a
union of love: love, mercy, benevolence, goodness,
salvation, are banned from his discourse, as is, for that

matter, evil. The creation, and thus the procession of the manifold from the One, is ontologically necessary and the One, by being simple, is in a sense everything (not unlike the Christian God) (91 *bis*) or makes every created being One-everything (35). Strictly speaking, it is improper to say either that things proceed from the One or that they do not; the One does nothing and it is only the poverty of our language and thought which makes us say that the One creates: this creation is entirely different from anything we are able to grasp (39). Ultimately, neither the procession of things from the One – however many intermediary steps are needed to descend from it to matter – nor their final return to the One, occasionally mentioned (34), are within the reach of our concepts.

And it is the bizarre ambiguity of the One as we conceive of it – its creative non-self-sufficiency and its idle self-sufficiency combined – that compels Damascius to seek for another principle which needs nothing in any respect, is not even a principle, has no name and by no means, however indirect, can open unto us an insight into itself.

There is no proper word to give it. We may not say that it is higher than anything else, since 'to be higher' implies a relationship with something, whereas no relationship can be spoken of in this case. It is so ineffable that to call it ineffable is improper (24, 5, 444); for the same reason it is wrong to say that 'not to be conceivable' belongs to its nature (7); nor can it be known even by One, as by such a knowledge the One would split, and thus destroy itself (26). Not a cause, not a principle, this Eschaton is nothing; indeed, Damascius says it is the Nothing or the no-thing, not-being (7). Its inaccessibility is total and itself unspeakable; in the face of this super ignorance (Damascius' word: *huperagnoia* (29)) only absolute silence is recommended (5, 13). The key result is: among all improper words to name the Eschaton, the least improper is 'nothing'.

On several occasions (for instance 4, 7, 443) Damascius repeats his doctrine of two kinds of Nothing: there is a Nothing that is the first above everything, including the One and the Being, and a Nothing that is the lowest, the last and the worst, and this is what lies below matter (the latter seems to retain a shadow of being). Both prepositions 'above' and 'below' are inadequate, to be sure, as they involve an expressible relationship and therefore wrongly imply that the supreme or the *infime* Nothingness is, after all, negatively related to other levels of reality.

Having thus arrived at the top and the bottom of whatever is, and made the distinction between two sorts of nothingness, both utterly ineffable, Damascius falls into the very trap which it was his main purpose to avoid: he negatively defines what can never be, as he says, *negatively*, let alone positively, defined. The self-reference trap is unavoidably included in any attempt to speak of the unspeakable. To define something as undefinable is to deny that it is undefinable. To recommend 'the absolute silence' is to violate this very commandment.

Damascius wades further in self-contradiction. After having declared the total ineffability of the Eschaton and the perfect absence of all relations it might hold with anything else he asks (8) whether or not something of the most sublime Nothingness has come over to things, and to us. And he replies that there are indeed in us some of its vestiges; otherwise we would not be capable of having any thought of it in our mind. Everything, it turns out, participates in the Ineffable, in other words something ineffable is preserved in whatever there is. Moreover, having denied any causality that could be attributed to the Ineffable, he now clearly implies that everything proceeds from it.

And so the Nothingness is a 'principle', after all. That the impenetrable darkness is the name for the single principle – or beginning – of the universe, had been known to the Egyptian sages from whose secret teaching Damascius, as he claims (125 *quater*), took up his wisdom.

Damascius probably went further than any of his fellow Platonists in robbing the Eschaton of all person-like characteristics and in unfolding the inherent inconsistency of our minds when they deal with it: we are compelled to talk about it, because our minds cannot escape the desire to reach the utmost limits of being; and we are aware that all the words and images whereby we try to reach it are bound to be wrong. Since we know that all the words we might ever be capable of using in this description depend on contingent properties of the world of finite things, we come, after successive denials, to the idea of Nothingness as the least distorting name for the Absolute. When Damascius talks about the One, he avers that it is by definition, not-something; any name refers to something (29 *bis*) thus (presumably) to what can be identified by contrast to other 'somethings', whereas the One's nature cannot be negatively dependent on anything else's nature.

It may be safely said that Damascius, in the laboriously constructed chaos of his work, arrived at the notion which Hegel would subsequently sum up in this short sentence: the pure Being and the pure non-Being are the same. To be sure, Damascius made the just mentioned distinction between two levels of Nothingness, but this distinction is no more conceptually expressible than each of its terms severally.

DIVINE NOTHINGNESS IN CHRISTIANITY

The topic of divine Nothingness persisted among great Christian neo-Platonists once the One or the Ineffable of pagan ontologists had successfully - though indigestibly - swallowed up the biblical Father. The chief culprit was certainly pseudo-Dionysius, whoever he was. His role in shaping the philosophical history of christianity can hardly be over-estimated. It has been noticed more than once that if the author of *On Divine Names* had not been mistaken for centuries for whom he pretended to be - the first Bishop of Athens converted by St Paul (Acts, 17.54) - he most probably would not have got away with his brazen neo-Platonism and his work would have remained in the annals of Christian though as a heretical freak. This innocent literary hoax (or perhaps just act of modesty on the part of a humble monk who preferred to attribute his own intellectual achievements to a venerated figure of the past) slanted the course of the spiritual history of Europe. It ineradicably affected western Christianity with the spirit of Hindu and Buddhist wisdom, the impact of which, historians have suggested, is detectable in later Platonism, little as might have been known about the actual routes of its invasion into the Alexandrian and Athenean market of ideas. Pseudo-Dionysius clearly was not satisfied with simple assertions of God's ineffability. The latter had been a standard tenet of Christian faith. The sense of ineffability was changed significantly on the assumption that every word, uttered about God, is as proper as any other, and that, in fact, every word is improper; no theology is conceivable on this assumption: nothing can be meaningfully said about the Creator.

And he goes further. We are not allowed to say about God that he has reason or intelligence, that he lives or is life, or substance, truth, spirit, wisdom, One and unity; indeed he is nothing of those things which exist or do not exist (*Myst. Theol.*, chapter V; *De Divinis Nominibus*, chapter V). More orthodox commentators, starting with St Maximus the Confessor, used to explain Dionysian excesses as an innocent repetition of the notion that God is 'above everything'. But this is a distorting reduction. If it is wrong to say that 'He is' or that He is One, Truth and Life and if, consequently, Christian faith is beyond intelligible expression, we are left with the contemplation of Nothingness as the only form of belief. Certainly, we have the Holy Writ, and Dionysius warns us indeed (*De Div. Nom.*, chapter I.2) that we must not say or think anything about God beyond this message. This is a shaky and dubious compromise between Christianity and neo-Platonism: we have, on the one hand, in the world of concepts, the nameless abyss of Nothingness and, on the other, the sacred text which it is illicit to interpret, even mentally, and which is frozen in its purely verbal surface and thus unintelligible.

A number of medieval and later Christian speculative mystics took up Dionysian themes. They include Nicholas of Cusa who avers, in the same, characteristically neo-Platonic manner, that, Truth being incommunicable (since it coincides with God), no word, even 'ineffable' may be properly assigned to God; if he cannot be called 'nothing' this is because 'Nothing' is a name as well (*Nihil non est, quia hoc ipsum nihil nomen habet nihili - Dialogus de Deo Abscondito*) but neither may we name him 'something', the latter word being applicable to particular beings only. God is then '*supra Nihil et aliquid*' and avowedly inexpressible faith slips into an act of worship without an identifiable object. Perhaps the most suggestive and concise summary of this doctrine is given in the well-known epigram of Angelus Silesius: 'God is verily nothing and insofar as he is something, he is thus only in me, as he chose me for Himself' (*Cherubinischer Wandersmann*, I, 200).

We know from the studies of Gershom Scholem (cf. his '*Ueber einige Grundbegriffe des Judentums*, 1976) that the same puzzle – how to melt into one the biblical Father and the neo-Platonic Absolute – was to plague Jewish medieval thought as well, culminating occasionally in the notion – as adventurous as melancholic – of the supreme Nothing.

The logic of this Nothingness theology seems hardly avoidable once it has been decided that the Lord of the Christian and Jewish traditions is indeed the Absolute. A theologian, having paid tribute to the principle of God's ineffability but talking about him at length nonetheless, is often coerced into the admission that God, sharing no properties with his finite creatures and being in no way identifiable – even negatively – within a discourse that fits only into the world of things, is necessarily not-something or no-thing. And here the language breaks.

ON ALL POSSIBLE LANGUAGES (1)

The language might have, indeed, suffered a nervous breakdown, but this is, we may expect, not a terminal sickness. It will probably resume its never-ending attempt to cross its own borders and venture into the illicit realm of the unspeakable. We live, no doubt, in a civilization which sets strongly guarded barriers around our use of words, but, naturally enough, brings to life a number of new ways and tricks designed to cheat the wardens. We are not sure where the invincible ghost of the Absolute is going to re-emerge from and how it will come back to life. It might loom up from quite unexpected corners, for instance from the razor-sharp minds of physicists and mathematicians, and there are some signs that it is trying, tentatively, to sneak through those royal doors. It might even attempt to elbow its way, stealthily, through the contemporary philosophical divinization of language. Once we have a gospel of which the Prologue may be summed up briefly: 'God is just a Word but the Word is God', once it turns out that the language is divinely self-constituted and thus self-validating and that what words are about is words, we may at least believe that in terms of meaningfulness (or its absence), the words 'God', and the 'Absolute' do not differ from 'apple' and 'mountain'. This might turn out to be the oblique, though painful, route through which God and the Absolute will re-assert their legal presence in our tongue and the word will become flesh again. The same may be said about the pragmatic mentality which enjoys, or so it appears, a fairly robust health in the philosophical kingdom. Pragmatic thinking, including the utilitarian notion of truth, was supposed to free us from the fetters of meta-physical speculation, by measuring validity by usefulness. But it is easy to see that the concept of usefulness, however conceived – narrowly or generously, psycho-logically or socially – opens a wide gate through which the same metaphysics and theology can triumphantly return and assert their legitimacy, for one need only argue that they might be at the service of some human needs. Epistemological relativism of various kinds – more often than not designed to kill metaphysics for ever – falls prey to the same simple trap: it can legalize anything, including the same metaphysics, but its followers are rarely ready to admit it.

This is admittedly no more than speculation. But to expect the Absolute will let itself be permanently exiled from human spiritual life is probably a wishful thought of die-hard empiricists. We cannot help being time-producers and thus self-destroyers. We cannot help feeling that whatever has happened is not there any more and, therefore, we are inclined to suspect, is not real: our joys and sufferings and ultimately ourselves, have no *esse* of their own and consequently no *esse* at all. This most common feeling, variously expressed for centuries by poets, philosophers, religious thinkers and mystics is probably irrepressible, much as it might be dismissed as irrelevant to any practical or scientific worries. The quest for the Absolute both expresses this feeling and suppresses it; it displays human anxiety in the face of the experience of the irreality of the word, the feeling that *Alles Vergängliche ist nur ein Gleichnis*, and it invalidates, so to speak, this very experience by pointing at the Being which is bound to be, which is timeless and One and which generously restores to being the fragile world of experience and makes everything miraculously real again.

And in the very moment we achieve this result – or believe we do – it seems to crumble because the Absolute is sucked away into the bottomless pit of ineffability.

Once we look back at our route, we notice how close we are to Damascius' double Nothingness.

Time, as a substratum of human experience, cannot be conceptualized (in the sense: reduced to more primitive terms). If time is perceived as an endless self-annihilation, the entire world of experience lacks the substratum and sinks into nothing. The Absolute is supposed to redeem the world, to save it from the never-beginning and never-ending death: in its eternal present everything is preserved, everything protected and made permanent, nothing ever perishes; it produces the ultimate support for the existence of anything, it embodies the final subjugation of time. To perform this function, however, it has to be not only immune to time but perfectly self-contained and indivisible; therefore we can never know how the (apparent) Nothingness of the universe is restored to the glory of being in the Eschaton's perennial unity, without blasting this unity asunder. And since the Absolute, like time – its defeated but living foe – cannot be conceptually reduced to anything else, its name, if there is one, is Nothing. And so, a Nothing rescues another Nothing from its Nothingness.

This is *horror metaphysicus*.

Risum teneatis. Mankind, in all the variety of its civilizations, has never been, and probably will never be, able to escape from its desire to escape from time. If the cultural expression of this craving is stripped of mythological symbols and is supposed to have achieved an abstract exactness, a literal perfection, it collapses into paralysing muteness. This is not to say that the desire is not genuine or that the desperate attempts to give it an articulated shape in terms of this horror have to be dismissed. It is perhaps better for us to totter insecurely on the edge of an unknown abyss than simply to deny its presence by closing our eyes.

We cannot have any certainty about the hidden potential of language. It is not believable and hardly believed any longer that our language is entirely parasitic on common perception: if it were, people could probably have elaborated arithmetical and geometrical techniques but how could they ever have arrived at the integral calculus, Cantor's numbers and the non-Euclidean geometries? Mathematics is the most powerful intellectual vehicle, ever devised, whereby we escape from time. But there is no reason to expect that it ever might arrange the kind of escape which the quest for the Absolute has embodied. For centuries philosophers and religious thinkers have brutally stretched, tortured and raped the language, trying to extort from it its concealed riches. Many of those assaults proved to be dead-ended, yet some were not. Most probably people will never be satisfied with the inherited, ready-made stock of their tongue, and this not only for trivial reasons, e.g., because they have to baptize newly discovered and fabricated things, but because of the suspicion that the language, when pressed, might yield more than it is willing to admit to possess.

Let us repeat: insofar as the Absolute, in spite of its invincible elusiveness looms indistinctly on the horizon of all our possible languages, never pin-pointed, always gropingly sought, it cannot be, within the bounds of our wit, conceived of as a person or a god; no communication with it is possible or needed and it cannot be addressed 'Thou'. It is a rather symbolic entity, a powerless but extremely important constitutional monarch who provides the universe of things, minds, events and gods with a continuous ontic legitimacy, but who does not govern. Without it the *infime* Nothingness would reign supreme. The *Ultimum* explains nothing, if the word 'explain' retains its normal meaning; we cannot say in what sense it might endow anything with reality, truth or goodness, but it is perhaps a necessary condition on which anything can be real, true or good at all. On the assumption that the God-person is the real governor of his universe, he is not the Absolute – at least not in terms of what we can, however awkwardly, express. Hellenized Christian philosophy and some mystics say that he is both, for all our inability to make this identity clear. To say more, our minds would have to expand beyond their present borders and expand their linguistic resources correspondingly. Perhaps we ought not to be so bold as to state self-assuredly that this can never happen, that we have reached the uppermost barriers of experience and speech.

RECYCLING THE *COGITO* (2)

The axis of *horror metaphysicus*, we said, has two poles: the Absolute and the self or *Cogito*. Both are supposed to be bastions that shelter the meaning of the notion of existence. The former, once we try to reduce it to its perfect form, uncontaminated by contact with any less sublime reality, turns out to pass away into nothingness. The latter, on closer inspection, seems to suffer the same fate.

We tried to recycle the Cartesian *Cogito*, dismissing its ambitions as a font of all certitude, but retaining, for a moment, its possible use as a paradigm, perhaps an indispensable conceptual tool which makes intelligible the act of existence. The history of post-Cartesian discussion, up to our time, has revealed the fragility of this insight, and step by step pushed this second pivot of Reality down into the same conceptual void.

From the very beginning, one of the main targets of Descartes' critics was, of course, his careless transition from 'I think' to 'I am a thinking substance (or thing).' *Ego cogito* is a normal, correctly built and unsuspect sentence. 'Substance' was supposed to be what cannot be predicated on anything else and therefore the word was understandable only by contrast to 'accident', 'property', 'quality', etc. That 'I think' equals 'I am something that thinks' might be tautologically true but to deduce from the same premise 'I am a thing whose nature involves nothing but thinking' or 'I am a spiritual substance' seemed utterly impermissible to Gassendi and Hobbes. Indeed, Descartes did not deduce the separate substantiality of mind from the sheer *Cogito*. He rather averred that he could mentally grasp the act of *cogitatio* (the word embraced all conscious acts, the entire field of subjectivity) without necessarily presupposing the presence of the body. When the critics argued that the *Cogito* could by no logical means be transmuted into an independent substance and that the fact of thinking is quite compatible with the idea that thinking is no more than a function or a property of the body, they obviously stood on firm ground, but they missed the main point of Descartes' discovery, as subsequent discussion was soon to reveal.

It is uncontestable that *cogito* could be expressed only in the first person singular, indeed, that once converted into another grammatical form (Peter thinks, therefore Peter is) it would become an absurdity. Descartes himself explained (in response to the *Second Objections* to the *Meditations*) that, in spite of the *ergo* it involves, his formula was not a syllogism in which the major premise has been suppressed, but a single act of intuition. In other words: without being a sufficient ground to prove the presence of an immaterial soul which each of us is, the *Cogito* asserted the absolute irreducibility of acts of being conscious (or of 'subjectivity'); whatever happens to my body is public, so to speak, whereas the events consisting in my experiencing my body (or other realities) are not;

others might guess them and I can describe them but these events – perceptions, emotions, feelings, thoughts – remain for ever secluded within my incurable self-closure and they are immune to doubt. All this has been well-known, of course, to Cartesians and to anti-Cartesians alike and I do not intend to discuss various arguments purporting to demolish this discovery of the privacy of *cogitatio*. My purpose is not to support Descartes but to reflect upon the destiny of the *Ego-cogito*, upon historical quasi-fatality which ends in the disappearance of 'ego' as a separate conceptual unit.

When a Cartesian says that my experience is not accessible to others, he implies – and usually says – that it is accessible to *me*. This 'me' is thus automatically implied to be different from the very experience, and it is far from being immediately clear what it is, apart from the obvious fact of continuous memory and apart from the un-contested legitimacy of the pronoun 'I' in language (apparently some languages do without, though). One may try to dismiss the entire problem in the Humean fashion, but one cannot de-legalize the pronoun in a language where it established its right to stay. How is this right to be defined?

The authors of the *Sixth Objections* to the *Meditations* made at the very outset a modest and, at first glance, a not very enlightening remark: in order to say *Cogito ergo sum* Descartes must have previously known what *cogito* and *sum* mean. Descartes lightly sets this criticism aside by saying that everybody unreflectingly knows what is meant and that this knowledge is innate. On second thoughts, the objection is perhaps worth more attention. Everybody may indeed use the words *cogito* and *sum* without hesitation and with a feeling of understanding, but the very use of language is not innocent: every sentence we utter presupposes the entire history of culture of which the language we use is an aspect. No word is self-transparent. None may pretend to hand over to the hearer the unadulterated world to which it is supposed to refer. Whatever reality the word conveys, it is a reality filtered through the thick sediments of human history we carry in our minds, though not in our conscious memory. Therefore, by phrasing his immortal sentence, Descartes had no right to plead epistemological innocence, or 'presuppositionlessness' (an ugly and unnatural word, used in English translations of Husserl as perhaps the only possible equivalent to the sound German noun *Voraussetzungslosigkeit*). Assuming that there is a bottom-reality (whatever that means) and even that there is an experience whereby we touch it, the unique quality of this experience, its uncontaminated freshness, its being the divine beginning, is fatefully lost when it is dressed in words. Spoken of, the world is never naked.

ON HUSSERL

For the same reason, Husserl's brave attempt to salvage the *Cogito*, wrecked by sceptics, was doomed to fail, however ingeniously he might have tried to get rid of the spurious 'substantiality of ego' while keeping safe Descartes' genuine transcendental insight. Husserl was a Cartesian in that to him the question *par excellence* which makes philosophy worth doing at all is: what may and what may not be doubted? He dismissed ego as a 'substance'; it was, in his view, no more than a residue which Descartes wanted to retain after the world as a whole had been put under the interrogation mark. Once we suspend (or put into brackets) our natural belief in the existence of the world, the 'psychological ego' – as a 'substance' or as a series of events that occur in the world – has to be suspended as well. The world which remains is a collection of meanings to be investigated, not of things or events as we normally think of them. The transcendental ego, the pure absorber of meanings, cannot be a substance in any recognizable sense, both because it remains, along with the world, within the consciousness and because it is necessarily intentional, directed towards something else. The distinction between an act of cognition and its object has not been abolished but, since they both occur 'in consciousness', the object can become transparent, even if the process of interrogating and interpreting it is infinite. Once Descartes manufactured a substance from the act of thinking, he could imagine that this mind, a parcel of the universe, does not need to extend itself, in a movement of intention, towards an object; it is simply there, whether or not it projects itself; it arrives at self-assurance in the act of self-knowing. To Husserl, however, ego is not an immobile thing: to be directed to something is an unremovable property of its constitution.

'Substantiality' having been thus done away with, it is not at all clear what has been saved by Husserl from the ego and what is ego-ist in this relic; neither do we know what is conscious in the transcendentally reduced consciousness that embraces both poles: the purified subject of cognition and the infinite universe of meanings, each of those poles being necessarily coupled with the other. Ego seems to be no more than an empty recipient of de-realized phenomena or a sheer movement of intention, an act without actor.

This new philosophical faith was supposed, once again, to guide us towards the epistemological eschaton, to an absolutely original spring of knowledge; that knowledge presupposed nothing except itself and it was, consequently, as necessary as God. Yet the price to be paid for this discovery was exorbitant; save the name, 'I' disappeared and the universe was reduced to meanings, springing ultimately from this very 'I': two no-things supporting each other. We have reached the cognitive Absolute by emptying it of reality.

Uneasiness in the face of those conclusions was widely felt and it resulted less in new attempts to resume the path towards the same goal and more in renouncing the goal itself or in explaining that both Descartes' and Husserl's questions were wrongly shaped. Heidegger did not ask about the unconditioned beginning of knowledge, he did not talk of consciousness, sense-data, substantiality or non-substantiality of ego or transcendental suspension of the reality of the world. He did not define the human phenomenon in either psychological or cognitive terms: he accepted it as being invincibly contingent, thrown in a contingent situation, incapable of running away from the world by mental effort. Human existence, ever mine, can be described in its various relationships towards itself, towards others and the world, but it cannot be defined in more primitive terms; it is an ontological, not psychological or empirical fact, and there is nothing ultimate in it, no source of certainty about itself or God or the universe.

ON MERLEAU-PONTY

Merleau-Ponty attempted to show more specifically what was wrong with both the Cartesian and the Husserlian *Cogito*. He argues (against Descartes and in agreement with Husserl) that the act of a purely self-directed *Cogito* simply cannot occur, as a matter of fact. This amounts to saying that no purely 'inner person' is given in our experience. I cannot think of myself without discovering myself in the world. This is because by no mental or intellectual feat can I invalidate or cancel perceptions, and my finite perceptions reveal a cognitive power which is co-extensive with the world and discloses it step by step. If I lack certainty about things, I cannot be certain about my perception either, for the affirmation of the world is included in the perception, instead of being added to it in a separate intellectual act; if I grasp my own *cogitatio* with certainty, the world which it aims at is embedded in it. In other words, my own existence cannot be reduced to the awareness of this existence. Besides, Descartes, according to this criticism, neglects the mediating role of language: his *Cogito* is expressed in words and I acquire the ability to use words by learning how people manipulate them in the context of a given situation, not unlike the way I learn to use tools.

If Husserl was right in abandoning the non-intentional *Cogito*, the pure self-grasping interior without object, his own idealist way to wrestle with the Cartesian problem failed as well, in Merleau-Ponty's view. If it is the transcendentally reduced ego which sets up (constitutes) the world, one may not assume that only essences, and not hyle – the matter of the world – are included in those creative acts. Not to be able to suspect or annul the perception amounts to not being able to suspend the world. In reality my very act of existence is nothing but the movement of 'transcending' myself, and any act of self-reflecting is to be seen within that movement.

It is indeed arguable that if it were true that I have no unmediated access to anything save myself and if, consequently, the existence of others were cancelled or forever doubtful or inconceivable or reduced to artefacts of the almighty transcendental consciousness, the very fact of communication and the possibility of language, including the language wherein the *ego cogito cogitata mea* or *die Voraussetzungslosigkeit* appear, would be unintelligible and unaccountable.

And so, Merleau-Ponty took up the Heideggerian 'to-be-in-the-world' as a first, non-negotiable datum, not to be explained any further, even though he believed that Heidegger's insight was possible only against the background of the transcendental reduction which they both felt compelled to dismiss. Ultimately he seemed to assume – without saying so in so many words – that the question of the 'existence' of the world is not so much solved or soluble or insoluble but rather wrongly asked – by Descartes and Husserl alike. We are simply never in the position to start this kind of interrogation, as the very act of asking requires that we reach a place which is prior to the perception and language.

Since he assumed, however, that perception and the world unfold together, as it were, so that the question of their respective priority makes no sense, he should have concluded that the very question of truth in a traditional sense or *adaequatio* makes no sense either. But then, naturally enough, he had to cope with the question of how the erroneous or illusory perception is conceivable at all. Merleau-Ponty discarded the question too easily by saying that we may have doubts about one or another part of the world but not about the whole, fragments of which disclose themselves in acts of perception. Here, however, he seems to be entangled in a snare of his own making, considering that no 'whole' is an object of perception and, therefore, to affirm the whole is an intellectual act of assertion and not a perception. The priority of perception is thus invalidated; if perception (which includes the world) is absolutely prior, it should be by definition infallible, as in Epicurus. If it may be corrected, another tribunal, equal to, or higher than, perception is needed. It would probably not be out of keeping with Merleau-Ponty's intention to say that this court of appeal is indeed present in the very communication between people, that is to say, truth or *adaequatio* is ultimately decided by the verdict of a speaking community. This pragmatic solution, apart from the doubts concerning the self-reference paradox it involves, would make void the privileged rank of perception.

Those arguments are cited as links in the process which was to end with the annihilation of ego as a foundation (conceptual, not only experimental) of the very intelligibility of existence.

The late nineteenth-century empiriocritics who assailed the Cartesian projects argued – on Humean lines – not only that spiritual 'substance' is a dispensable figment but that the very distinction between mental and physical events is no more than a convenient fiction, having no ontological sense. Whether an event is described as mental or physical depends on which of its characteristics we intend to grasp; whether physical phenomena are mind-made or the other way round – mental states are a special category of physical events – is a question improperly stated. We know neither a pure mental, self-related and self-asserting interior or an experience which would be no-one's experience. We know the world as an infinite flow of experience which we arrange according to various criteria – like time, space and substance – for practical purposes. And that is enough both for science and daily life. Ontological questions are invalidated, and we are not in the position to ask legitimately 'what is the world really?', 'what is the stuff the world is made of?' and the like. Both ego and material substance pass into a void except when they are employed as artificial tools in reasoning; only specific, empirically soluble (or mathematical) questions may be legally asked, and the truth as a relationship between the-world-in-itself and our perception or knowledge is cast off as a residue of metaphysical prejudices. The Cartesian fallacy disappears and so does the ego.

A digression might be useful in this place. Gilson, who devoted so much effort to the recreation of the genuine 'existential' meaning of St Thomas' natural theology and to the refutation of Kantian or Cartesian distortions in interpreting it, argued that the whole intuition of God is focused, in Thomist (and his own) terms, on the pure act of existing, rather than of creating. The 'I am who I am' is God's title *par excellence* and, of course, chosen by himself. Christian philosophers who (like the Cartesians, including Malebranche) define God by the idea of perfection and infer from this definition his necessary existence, rather than the other way round, are guilty of producing a strange discrepancy between the God of philosophy and the God of religious revelation. The essence of the Christian God is 'to be' and not 'to create' or 'to be infinite'. The oblivion of the act of existing is, according to Gilson, the main source of aberration in philosophical modernity. He remarks, however, that this removal of existence probably resulted from the simple fact that the notion of existence, while perfectly simple, cannot be conceptualized.

This is perhaps the most distressing point in the entire history of philosophical debate on the Absolute. If indeed intuition of the act of existing is both perfectly simple and perfectly resistant to all attempts at conceptually expressing its content we should simply be satisfied with accepting it as it is, as an irreducible and primitive insight which everybody is naturally ready to understand. But if there were such an insight it would be strange that it could have ever been forgotten. Assuming – which is perhaps Gilson's contention – that it was philosophers who, by trying to analyse what is unanalysable, tore asunder and eventually killed this primitive intuition, can their destructive work be undone? If so, then probably not by further intellectual mediation but rather by the outright dismissal of philosophy.

EGO AS A QUASI-ABSOLUTE

Nobody nowadays scours the mind and universe for the elusive Grail of unshakeable certainty, and it is generally assumed that all the discoveries made in that quest – whether *Cogito*, Husserl's eidetic insight, or the Viennese protocular sentences – have turned out to be fake. We cannot return to pre-cultural, pre-linguistic, pre-historical – that is to say pre-human – cognitive innocence and still continue to use our philosophical idiom to depict it. But *Cogito*, through its advocates and critics alike, changed the route of intellectual history. Certainly, by Descartes' time 'the inner man' was a well-established tenet of religious and mystical writing. It was reinforced by Luther's theology of faith and by many prophets of the 'inner word' who both followed and rebelled against him. Yet, instead of vindicating irreducible 'subjectivity', this trend was to crush it. It took up and radicalized the Augustinian attack on self-will as the seed of evil. On the other hand, the 'inner man', the only one to be saved or damned, was opposed to the man of flesh in antiecclesiastical terms: the point was to scrap all 'external' means of salvation – works, institutional help, priesthood, ceremonies, temples and rituals. On the other, the supreme task of the inner man was to discover in himself the divine Word – or simply God – to annihilate his own will and to arrive at the state of perfect passivity. And so, the inner man attained his fullness by throwing himself away. He looked into himself only to find God, rather than himself. Descartes, however, discovered the inner world not in order to transubstantiate it into the divine ground of being; it was supposed to be the final step itself. It revealed the only world that was self-transparent and therefore as self-identical as the Absolute but, unlike the Absolute, directly accessible and not the result of abstract reasoning.

The Cartesian ego is indeed an absolute in the sense that, being unique and exclusive every time, self-closedly and self-reflectedly mine, it may always say, like the biblical creator 'I am who I am'. 'I' am the pure actuality because in every 'now' I am everything I can be. This consequence of *Cogito* was not disclosed by Descartes who almost entirely left its time-dimension aside; he knew time only as a framework of physical events, not as a life-form of spirit. Bergson unfolded the ego as a movement of real time or as a time-generating energy. So conceived, ego is a pure actuality like the absolute, but for the opposite reason: if the neo-Platonic One is always actual, and no potentialities are concealed in it, this is because it is a perfectly self-confined immobility; ego instead is mobility itself: it is a continuous event whose continuity is assured by an incessantly growing stock of memory. In concrete time, i.e., time in which the distinction between now and then, and not only between earlier and later, obtains, whatever is real is real only now; consequently potentiality can never be real. We talk about something being potential to the extent that we look at an object or a state of affairs as having already gone into the past – whether it has thus effectively gone or we project our minds into a moment that has not yet arrived and locate ourselves, by an effort of imagination, in the future. In the reality of now – that is to say in the only 'real reality' – everything is actual. Ego, though uninterruptedly in movement, is self-identical in every 'now' and therefore self-identical *tout court* (unlike in neo-Platonic time which makes self-identity impossible).

Being self-identical like the Absolute, ego is, like the Absolute, though for opposite reasons, unique and necessary. It is unique in that it may never, in contrast to all other empirical entities, be grasped as a specimen of a genus, as 'something' of which two or more examples can fall under a general concept. There is no concept of 'I' – a point which Kierkegaard made emphatically. Being accessible only to myself, 'I' have no content to share with anything else and therefore no conceptual means of producing a universal that would embrace both myself and an alter-ego. The Absolute is unique because it is infinite, limitless, impassible and timeless; 'I' am unique because I am the limit itself, the pure temporality. And why I am necessary is not because the very *idea* of 'me' excludes my non-being or my having an origin but because, being known solely to myself, I am unable to conceive of either my absence or the cause which brought me into existence.

The Cartesian ego is a kind of black hole: it can suck in anything (except for an alter-ego) and nothing can escape from it. Ineffable and incommunicable, conceptually unconstructible, it may be properly called nothing (indeed, they tell us now in Oxford that the word 'I', while having a meaning, has no reference.)

ON DE-CARTESIANIZATION

We are tempted to perceive, retrospectively, a fateful historical necessity in the way the Cartesian world, after having been halved into two hopelessly incommunicable parts – the point-like self and the homogeneous, infinite and infinitely divisible space – was to be appropriated in subsequent centuries. The evasive ego, an indifferent and inexplicable observer of matter, became irrelevant for all theoretical purposes and it was easily and serenely junked by those who focused their curiosity upon a world that one could investigate, understand and describe in abstract concepts; scientism and materialism took up – legitimately – one hemisphere (western? left?) of the Cartesian legacy. The other hemisphere was taken – legitimately – by those who started with *Cogito* and inevitably remained in it forever; they either suspended the universe in a precarious state of serfdom under the domination of ego or even made of it an ego's creation.

By tearing asunder reality Cartesianism was brought to self-denial; there was no room for mind in the space, and the eternally virgin self, the pillar of knowledge, evaporated. If it tried to convert itself onto the whole and to enslave matter, it became Nothing again (from Fichte to Husserl).

To be sure, parts of the broken Cartesian world keep living to some extent. The so-called 'discovery of subjectivity' (whether discovery or creation is another matter) has persisted as an inalienable item in the heritage of modernity. It displayed its vigour in the nineteenth and twentieth centuries every time people revolted against 'the tyranny of universality' and opposed it with the refractory self-assurance of the indissoluble 'I-hood', whether the universality was conceived of in Hegelian,

Husserlian, or scientistic fashion: Kierkegaard, Schestov or, among our contemporaries, Levinas, may be seen in this perspective. Both scientism and anti-scientistic resistance, however, have been drawing energy from the divided stream of the same source which proved incapable of surviving as a whole, and both contributed, from opposite sides, to the de-Cartesianization of the world.

There are, of course, other de-Cartesianizing endeavours. Some physicists (like David Bohm) now try to rediscover (or to re-inject) mind in matter, to reanimate the dead corpus of the universe and to arrange its *disiecta membra* again into a living whole, as it was in various ancient, medieval and Renaissance cosmologies. They argue that the concept of a Whole-in-each-part has been made legitimate again by quantum physics, thus providing an unexpected link between modern science and the traditions of Hindu, Taoist and Buddhist wisdom, and moreover, that the Whole has mind-like properties. The Whole-in-part (an obvious absurdity in terms of Cartesian and Newtonian physics), apart from having been an intuition of most of the Absolute-seekers – emphatically so in Proclusian metaphysics – has always been present, in one way or another, in religious worship, including in many archaic beliefs. It is enough to have an idea, however vague, of an indivisible and creative deity to assume that this deity, being present in its works, cannot but be present in totality in each of them, thus defying commonsense geometry. And why indeed should the deity be constrained by Euclid's axioms? And if the omnipresent whole is real, it cannot be a material entity in any conceivable sense and appears to be a kind of intelligence. This does not imply that it is a self-conscious person. It might still be a primordial calculating device, the pure mathematic (or the pure logic) inscribing itself

70

into the world (a suggestion made by Paul Davis in *God and the New Physics*) or a Spinozan god who does not care about human affairs but has infallible computing power over the whole of creation. In this holistic perspective we are entitled to believe that matter is potentially mind not only in the trivial sense (if mind emerged from matter, then obviously matter must have been capable of producing it) but in that mind is actually present in all its varieties. Scientists who reason along those lines do not share the Humean or Machean belief (supported by the Niels Bohr, among the great physicists of our age) that physics is not a reproduction of reality but rather a schematization of experience with the aid of artificially concocted conceptual instruments. If the presence of the observer cannot be removed from the description of some physical events, this does not necessarily imply that the observer is a Kantian intellect that imposes a priori forms onto the shapeless stuff of perception: it is rather an intellect that discovers its own patterns in the reality as it verily is, and is able to reveal them because the reality is mind-like, and the very act of cognition, as Plato would have it, presupposes an affinity, or even a loving kinship, between my mind and the mind of the world.

Bernard d'Espagneat in his book *In Search of Reality* discusses these issues in a way which appears to the layman more cautious than that of some other metaphysicists; his discussion is focused as well on the concept of physical non-separability. If non-separability implies, he argues, that in some experimentally proven cases, particles which once interacted continue to interact, irrespective of distance, this suggests either that their non-separability is not a real fact but merely a way of describing the experiment (i.e. it has only an operational value) or that signals can sometimes travel faster than light. He thinks, however, that the unpleasant dilemma (to discard either the concept of reality or the relativity theory) is not insuperable if we accept instead the concept of non-local reality, thus ruining the notion of real space. The particles, investigated by a physicist, are not, in terms of contemporary quantum theory, real 'things' but temporary properties of a field. The strictly realistic interpretation of physics being, according to d'Espagnat, implausible, he opts instead for a non-physical realism; the world, described in quantum physics, is to be seen from this perspective as an aspect – next to, and complementary to, consciousness – of a veiled reality which is not bound by time and space as physics conceives them, and which he does not mind being called God. Those two inseparable sides of experience – the universe and consciousness – would be related to the ultimate reality which cannot be defined in terms of any scientifically valid experience.

The present author has no competence whatever to intervene in reflections, however metaphysical in content, which scientists make on the basis of their special knowledge or to assess the soundness of their interpretation. I do not know whether or not some differential equations and numerical relationships are effectively embedded in the universe rather than being imposed on it, and I suppose that the question is not, strictly speaking, within the realm of physics as it defines itself. Let us be satisfied with saying: the very act of knowing, the very fact that our mind communes with the world which it is not and that it can assimilate this world or make of it a self-conscious event, this most common fact, if we look at it without prejudice, is the strangest thing one can imagine. If God, as is said, is incomprehensible, the fact of perceiving and knowing is no less incomprehensible – at least on the common (and Cartesian) assumption that I am an observer of the universe which is radically, irreducibly alien. The 'mine–ness' might be a miracle but the fact of my making mine a foreign body, not previously present in me but converted into an act of awareness, is a miracle of miracles. Once we think of it we even feel a temptation to yield to the Platonic-Augustinian theory of anamnesis: that we know only what has always been in us. This is one of the ways in which we can approach the Whole-in-the-part insight: the Whole is in us and this is the reason why we can come to know anything at all.

ON SPINOZA

That the indivisible Whole – or the Absolute – is 'in' particular things, and therefore in each of us, is a tenet that appears, variously phrased, in the works of nearly all Platonists, including Plotinus, Proclus, Damascius, Eckhart and Nicolaus of Cusa, however difficult and awkward it might have been to make this idea compatible with the notion of the self-contained One. We find it even in Spinoza who had to cope with formidable, almost intractable, problems when he tried to express this view in his basically Cartesian idiom, designed for an entirely different purpose. While denying that the *esse* of substance belongs to the human essence (*Ethica*, II, Prop. 10 and Schol.), he states that particular things, i.e. 'modifications' or 'affections' of God, 'express' Him (I, 25, Cor.). The body and its idea are the same thing, differently seen, as, he observes, some Jews vaguely (*quasi per nebulam*) perceived by saying that God, God's intellect and things which are encompassed in His intellect are the same. He even avers that the human mind is

73

part of God's infinite intellect (II, 11, Cor.), even though God, being indivisble, can obviously have no parts (I, 13), and that the eternal intellectual love of God of which we are capable is a part of God's infinite self-love (V, 26). That all things are 'in' God is to him axiomatically true and that God cannot be 'in' things is no less obvious, as in this usage 'in' refers to absolute dependence. And so, without being able to speak of God's presence 'in' us, he sees human beings – and all beings, for that matter – as God's modifications or affections, notwithstanding the fact that substance, being impassible, immutable and indivisible, cannot be 'modified' or 'affected' in the sense of being changed by actions of finite individuals. The apparent contradictions are soluble, though, on the assumption that every particular thing is indeed God 'modified' or God expressing himself. In other words, Spinoza seems to repeat, in a modernized dialect, the same intuition which Eckhart explained by talking about the spark of divinity in us or about God's birth in the soul and which Cusanus tried to grasp by naming the world *explicatio* (in the sense of unfolding) of God and God *complicatio* of the world (coiling, furling). God is like a point in a line: everywhere present, never divided, always one. Atman is Brahman.

Unlike the Platonists of old, the pseudo-Cartesian of Amsterdam (pseudo because no trace of *Cogito* or 'subjectivity' was retained in his theology) did not think that the absolute was ineffable. He seemed to be satisfied with the riches of his language. The empiricist and rationalist critique was soon to shatter his laboriously built monument of 'geometrical' method. The train of modernity was fatefully driving towards the same abyss of double Nothingness: both the One and the *Cogito* were being converted, step by step, into *nihilum*. Surely, neither has ever disappeared completely. Metaphysics – in the sense of a search for the self-rooted Being – has survived, pushed down to a kind of demi-monde of philosophical life. Its language has been largely delegalized.

ON JASPERS (2)

It was Jaspers, among our contemporaries, who, perhaps better than anybody else, tried to face the seemingly final demise of both ultimate terms of human experience – the Absolute and self-referring existence – while rejecting the scientistic meaning of this demise. That the specifically human, each time unique, existence – in contrast to the biological, social, physical or psychological fact for which it must not be mistaken – is beyond the grasp of language, had been explained by Kierkegaard. That both existence and the Absolute, on closer inspection, dissolve into void, had been the stubborn contention of the Enlightenment. Jaspers took note of those results – irreversible, as he seemed to believe – of modernity, yet refused to accept their empiricist foundation and empiricist sense. The empirical reality, he insisted, is not self-explanatory or self-sufficient; the world does not offer us its own understanding. The visible, or scientifically elaborated universe which includes man as an object among objects is stretched between two realities – neither of which can be depicted in the language of knowledge – Transcendence and Existence. Those ultimate realities do not let themselves be objectified, appropriated by science, met in an inner-worldly experience. They are coupled inseparably with each other, that is to say, Existence (or freedom, or myself) is necessarily related to Transcendence (or the Encompassing) and the latter is there only for Existence.

75

They make two sides – one objective and one subjective – of the same reality which cannot ever become a positive achievement of intellectual effort, of an aesthetic, emotional or religious intuition, and which nonetheless is elusively hinted at and unspeakably present in all those fields of experience. This reality is not simply relegated into the realm of the absolutely Unknowable or of pure negativity, for what is hopelessly unknowable is of no interest and no relevance to our lives, whereas the awareness of what lies beyond the pale of knowledge is to Jaspers of the utmost importance and radically alters our attitude to the world. Everything takes on a new meaning once we perceive our experience as a phenomenon of the Eschaton, even though there is no method whereby the properties of the Eschaton could be inferred from the ways of its appearance. Although never grasped, the All-encompassing is a soil wherein human dignity is rooted; without attempts to leap over the barrier of the 'objectifiable' universe we could not overcome the feeling that our life is pointless. However unsuccessful, however unable to conquer death and defeat, those attempts are not futile: indeed, they make us human.

And so Jaspers yielded in his own way to the pressure of the Enlightenment, at least of Enlightenment in its empiricist, naturalist and utilitarian variant: as far as language and positive knowledge are concerned, both terms of the *Ultimum* – the divine and the human – were swallowed up by the Nothingness. They have been salvaged, all the same, not only as an indifferent limit of experience but as a reality to which the world of experience gives a way of evincing itself. Philosophical faith could preserve a shadow of the *Ultimum* but at a price of robbing itself of content: this faith seems to be sheer will to confront the All-encompassing, it has no means to convert itself into a word. No positive metaphysic, let alone theology, is reliably constructible and no revelation is credible; there is no voice of God in the world: if it were there, it would be irresistible, Jasper says.

Why so? Many people feel that God's voice is in the world and that it *is* irresistible; they say that if others do not hear it, this is because they refuse to do so; in other words God's voice is not mechanically irresistible, it is unmistakably audible to everyone who does not clog his ears.

Certainly, even those who listen to and are capable of decoding God's call, have to admit that it is perceived differently from, say, the light of the sun; and the difference consists in that the reality of sunlight is not a matter of contention among people. Those who discern divine signs in the world do not differ in empirical matters from those who fail to see them, but they do differ in the interpretation of experience. The interpretation of the former is simply declared illicit and meaningless by the latter according to the rules of language they have chosen to adopt. The question is therefore: are there any higher rules which we may use in making our choice among all possible languages?

LEIBNIZ AND ALL POSSIBLE WORLDS

It appears that no such rules are available. If they were to be binding in the same sense as logical rules are, they would have to be expressed in language, thus sucking themselves into the infinite regression.

According to Leibniz, God makes the choice among infinitely numerous, logically possible worlds. Each world is possible as long as its existence does not involve a

77

logical contradiction, because the principle of contradiction binds God no less than it does us. In surveying all the possible worlds, God is guided by his omniscience, but the effective choice is determined by his goodness: if he picks up the world in which the global amount of the good is optimally large by comparison with the mass of evil, this is because he is not only a mathematician who calculates and contrasts the respective properties of possible worlds, but a benevolent father as well. Perhaps (this is my, not Leibniz's comment) the Devil, or at least the chief of Satanic hordes, ex-seraph, would be able to perform a similar computation, but his choice would be, of course, opposite: he would choose a world of maximum evil. This amounts to saying that Leibniz's God is not the Absolute in the Platonic sense. It is impossible, or so it appears, to deduce the effectively existing world from perfect, all-embracing mathematics and logic – and this is what Leibniz otherwise suggests. In other words, there is no *mathesis universalis* that would abrogate the distinction between contingency and necessity, between *vérités de fait* and *vérités nécessaires*. This distinction inevitably appears, according to Leibniz, in the mind, because of the mind's limitation: we simply realize that to deny some truth (say, 'if a sentence p makes a sufficient condition for the sentence q, then the latter is a necessary condition of the former') results in contradiction, whereas to deny others (like 'Paul is a brother of Mary') does not. In a perfect mind, however, this distinction does not hold, as such a mind would see the necessity of all seemingly contingent events, all of them being included in the very concepts of things to which those events happen, or, to put it differently, a perfect mind knows that all truths are indeed analytical. This reasoning is undermined by the fact that God's kindness, not only his omniscience, had to be involved in deciding which of the possible worlds would become real. Therefore, in respect to God's omniscience, the world we live in *is* contingent. Leibniz could counter this objection by pointing out that God is good by definition and, consequently, to imagine a world which he has effectively chosen and which would not be the best possible is to contradict the Creator's benevolence; to deny any a priori valid definition would produce a contradiction: God was no less obliged to choose the best possible world than he was to create a world free of contradiction; he simply could not do otherwise.

There is a snag in this hypothetical counter-argument. Leibniz himself made a distinction in the *Theodicy* between metaphysical and moral necessity: God worked under metaphysical compulsion when he was creating a contradiction-free universe, and he also worked under moral compulsion insofar as his universe was the best possible in terms of the good/evil balance. It was possible to create a worse – or even the worst conceivable – world that would be logically consistent. Leibniz made God's omniscience and goodness independent from one another. Assuming that it was proper to infer God's necessary existence from the sheer fact of many possible worlds among which someone had to choose this one, rather than another, we know nothing about the reasons for this choice. Leibniz's proof of God's existence, if valid, says nothing about the creator's goodness and in itself does not exclude the terrifying possibility that he is actually a malevolent being; that he is not needs a separate proof which Leibniz failed to provide apart from assuming that goodness is an obvious part of perfection. But there is nothing compelling in this premise, since to prove the necessity of a creator, capable of choosing, is not a proof of his perfection if the latter by its very meaning includes goodness. God's metaphysical and moral qualities can be discussed separately. Moreover, the blasphemous idea might occur to us that God's goodness is contingent in respect of his omniscience (Leibniz does not say so, of course; neither does Duns Scotus who might have been responsible for Leibniz's separation of those two divine attributes). Once we start from this position, the proofs of God's existence leave the question of his goodness open; that he *is* good is simply accepted as a matter of course, as a part of the traditional concept, but this is by no means included in the logical chain of reasoning.

One might reply that there is nothing specifically Leibnizian or Scotist in this separation; after all, neither the ontological argument nor St Thomas' cosmological arguments directly imply God's necessary goodness; in their very content they do not bar the possibility of his being evil or a morally indifferent mathematician. St Thomas, after having proved God's perfection (in *Contra Gentiles*, I, 28), subsequently infers from it his goodness (37). To be perfect in the first sense seems to mean to achieve the highest possible degree in the given ladder of being but that the good is 'higher' than evil may be contested; Satan would, no doubt, contest it, and his logical skills are presumably not inferior to ours. Briefly, from the existence of God as a *primus movens, maxime ens, quo maius cogitari nequit*, etc. his goodness does not immediately follow; it calls for a separate argument and the latter is weaker than the proofs for a necessary being for reasons just mentioned: that perfection implies goodness is an arbitrary assumption; to proceed from the goodness of creatures to the kindness of their maker is not sound reasoning. If 'goodness' is an ontological characteristic, the argument would be credible only if it were true that being and goodness are co-extensive, and this metaphysical doctrine cannot be validated without previous knowledge of God's attributes and his unity; therefore the argument would be circular. And if 'goodness' is a moral quality, the circle would not arise but one would presuppose that human creatures are good as a matter of empirical observation which can be made apart from our knowledge of God. Yet they are clearly good in part and evil in part (assuming, for the sake of argument, that the sense of those adjectives is known to us) and it is far from obvious why our reasoning from the properties of derivative beings to the divine attributes should be necessarily based on the goodness, rather than wickedness, of the former.

Leibniz argues in addition (in *Principes de la Nature et de la Grâce*) that God has to have in eminent degree the qualities - or perfections - of his creatures, i.e., power, knowledge and goodness. This is an a posteriori argument which again requires the premise that perfection implies goodness (and why should there not be a perfection in evil?).

It might indeed be true that the logical separation of God's necessary existence from his benevolence was, in Leibniz's metaphysics, historically rooted in the very process which produced the need to *prove*, a priori or a posteriori, God's existence. St Thomas and even St Anselm can therefore be counted among the culprits. Once this need appears, we are almost under logical compulsion to separate God's being from his goodness, and make the latter a target of another demonstration, usually even more fragile and more fallible. Mystics attempted to heal this split but, much as they might have been venerated in the Christian tradition, they were witnesses rather than reasoners, intellectuals and proof-builders.

Certainly, neither Leibniz nor medieval thinkers can be blamed for taking for granted what had been a well-established biblical tradition that equated the ability to create with goodness; this tradition is not exclusively biblical; it appears in various, not necessarily monotheistic, mythologies. It is far from being omnipresent, though; in old Iranian myths and their Manichean off-shoots the malevolent God is a creator too, and one may argue that apart from the strength of the biblical heritage there are no firm grounds for such an equation.

ON CREATION, DIVINE AND HUMAN

The question is obscured by the confusion which the very word 'creation' carries. When divine creation is spoken of, creation *ex nihilo* is usually meant. But the concept 'ex nihilo' is a philosophical construct, having no unambiguous support in mythological imagery. God created heaven and earth, but does it clearly imply that, according to the Bible, there was literally nothing, apart from God, 'before' the first fiat? In this question a proviso is to be made, of course, for the improper use of the word 'before'; Christian theologies since St Augustine have been virtually unanimous in stating that time has been produced together with space and the universe, and thus it makes no sense to talk about a God who precedes the world in temporal terms. Physicists who now tell us that the universe emerged from a timeless and spaceless state seem to confirm that. Assuming, however, that creation *ex nihilo* was a privilege of a single Creator, nothing prevents us from imagining that in subsequent stages creative acts could have been performed both by God and by the Devil who used divinely supplied stuff in order to manufacture some creatures of his own for malicious purposes, for instance that God designed some friendly animals like horses, sheep and sparrows, and the Devil responded mischievously by inventing crocodiles, hyenas and cockroaches. If so, there is no necessary link between creation and goodness and no clear distinction between creating and destroying, between order and disorder; in human affairs creative efforts can be employed – or so we think – for evil purposes and an order can be at the service of the devil. If we deny that, we have to have other criteria for defining creation and order (why should not, for instance, the builders of the cruellest empires be called creators? Is not an extermination camp a kind of order, an organization? Cannot the artistic and intellectual creative labour of men be harnessed by demonic forces?) or to presuppose, as a matter of linguistic habit, that the words 'creation' and 'order' are applicable only to what we perceive as good; but then the 'good' may be either related to our moral feeling or to God who is good by definition.

As has been mentioned, the goodness of God used to be conceived as tripartite: as benevolence and love towards his creatures, as a source from which all rules of good and evil spring, and as an intrinsic goodness, independent from creative acts. In this last case goodness is simply interchangeable with being, so that God would be equally good even if, instead of creating the world, he had decided to remain in his indifferent loneliness; his goodness holds no recognisable relation to what we usually have in mind when using the word and therefore would appear incomprehensible to many people. If instead, according to the current usage, goodness implies loving benevolence and cannot be a priori identified with existence, and if it is assumed that the creator is unique, then diabolical or human ill will is capable only of destruction, whatever the appearances; the evil will can only spoil God's design, its seeming creativity is bringing nothing but chaos, disorder and havoc. The words 'order' and 'creation' are not neutral in respect to good and evil. They can only be used when a good purpose is meant. God's goodness is not self-related; it is naturally radiating – in accordance with St Thomas' famous formula '*bonum est diffusivum sui.*' To equate creation with the propagation of light – as in medieval light metaphysics – is conceptually natural.

This approach, traditional in Christian thinking, seems to entail the somewhat distressing idea that human beings are not capable of creation or that by boasting of our creativity we insolently arrogate to ourselves divine privileges.

Whether or not this consequence follows depends on what 'creativity' is supposed to be and what the meaning is of freedom of action which God, according to Christian faith, has endowed us with. If there is only one source of existence and of goodness, one source of energy, operating in all works of nature and of art, the concept of free will, to be retained, needs a lot of sophisticated effort; and in fact all the best minds in the history of European philosophy tried to elucidate this mystery (or to cancel it by decree). Without venturing into this infinite field of debate, we can be satisfied with one simple distinction.

The Augustinian doctrine implies that whenever we actually use our will – or our faculty of making a choice – we invariably use it against God; as a result of our self-induced corruption in original sin, we are never free in the sense of being able to choose between good and evil. If it is our own will that makes the decision, it chooses itself, that is evil. By choosing good we do not really choose; we rather renounce the choice in favour of the divine will that operates in us in the form of grace. It is assumed, however, that it was our own fault through which we lost the ability to make a free choice between good and evil; we were created free and therefore it may be fairly said that the irresistible propensity to evil did not belong to our pristine nature. After the fall there was nothing we could do to enable ourselves to perform good acts; only grace can restore this ability, but then the good we do is not ours.

This is admittedly a crude summary of St Augustine's teaching; to go into detail would require a lot of space and careful analysis. Still, it is good enough for my purposes.

In the Augustinian world it is not only the case that God is the ultimate source of all goodness – which is not controversial in Christian teaching – but also that we, human creatures, are not capable *post lapsum* of freely using this goodness to implement God's intentions. Among those who, at the outset of modern times, tried consistently to develop this doctrine, Luther was the most formidable. It was not a purely theological, theoretical question he wrestled with. He believed, it seems (an impression which his early writings, up to 1525, strongly convey), that we carry, all of us, an indestructible dark core in our being, a root of hell, which can never be tamed, never made innocent or employed for good purposes, never dissolved by the natural means at our disposal. No moral effort, no civilization, no virtues, no innate compassionate feelings can successfully fight against this Satanic kernel; it is just there, defying all our attempts to crush it (a concept that reminds one of the Freudian id which infallibly resists whatever civilization might do to domesticate it). It can only be annihilated by divine violence. Grace alone can destroy this seed of darkness in us, and if it works, it does so infallibly. Therefore, Luther strongly rejected the standard concept of the fifteenth-century nominalists, the concept of 'doing what is in one', *facere quod in se est*, as it presupposed that we had power to manipulate divine energy and thus to use our freedom to produce the good.

Within this world view human creativity is obviously unimaginable; whatever we do from our own initiative is fatefully evil, and evil, by definition, is pure negativity, pure destruction, a non-being.

But legitimate use of the idea of 'creation' looks more plausible once we locate ourselves within either the Catholic, minimalist, idea of freedom (as dogmatically defined by the Trent Council) or the generous and unlimited Cartesian notion which is in fact closer – as Descartes knew – to unphilosophical and untrained commonsense belief. In Catholic doctrine, while it is true that whatever good we are capable of is of divine origin and divine inspiration, it is not true that we are no more than passive objects of the operations of grace, because we are able, if we wish so, to turn our back on God and freely to scorn his offer. In other words, grace does not work irresistibly, which implies that our minimal positive co-operation – self-propelled readiness to accept grace – is involved in our morally relevant acts (if to forbear from the rejection of grace were caused by grace as a sufficient condition, we would be left with the same Lutheran concept, including probably its terrifying consequence: double predestination in the Calvinist sense).

Descartes deliberately and carefully avoided becoming entangled in theological disputes and therefore set aside, apart from a few remarks in the letters, sins and merits as aspects of human freedom. He was nonetheless clearly on the side of those who believed that freedom was the power of self-determination including the power to choose, without compulsion, between good and evil; indeed, in his famous private note he listed free will among the three great divine marvels next to the creation *ex nihilo* and God's incarnation as man. In terms of freedom of choice we do not differ from God, much as we differ in knowledge and power, both of which are relevant to our actual choices.

If we take seriously the idea of the good which human creatures can produce by self-causing moral acts – whether in the minimalist Catholic or in the illimited Cartesian version – there is a strong temptation to believe that those acts are really, and not metaphorically, creative. Assuming that the being and the good are co-extensive, it appears that by freely choosing the good we make the good actual and thus make actual the being in no less strong a sense than that acording to which we destroy the being by choosing evil. If each of us is a source of independent initiative which puts itself into movement and has no sufficient cause beyond itself, we seem to perform creative acts *ex nihilo*, to add to the being something that has not been there before, to nourish, to strengthen or to increase God.

Such a notion might seem blasphemous, heretical, idolatrous or all three from the standpoint of Christian-Platonist orthodoxy, as it undermines God's perfect actuality, omnipotence and his uniquely privileged power of creation.

It is no doubt true that if we try to reconcile this idea of creativity with everything we learn from perusing *Bullarium Romanum* and the decrees of Councils, we might get into trouble. But we apparently do not get into this kind of trouble when we read the Bible. The Bible's God is victim of all emotions, he is angry at, and frustrated with, the wayward manners of his subjects, but he loves them and he rejoices at seeing the kindness and obedience they display – albeit infrequently – in their lives. He is a god of love and he is a person in the same sense as we are.

The standard theologians' comment (most emphatically and repeatedly made in Maimonides' *Guide*) to the effect that the 'anthropomorphic' language of *Sacra Pagina* is adjusted to the meagre capacity of our minds, as they are unable to grasp the hidden metaphysical message, would be less doubtful if they – theologians, or at least some of them – did not pretend to have a dictionary whereby the divine word, as it stands, can be translated into the proper, exact idiom of their science. Apart from the claim to understand more fully what God really wanted to tell us, this attempt to explain the incongruity between myth and philosophy implies both that the myth is actually a philosophical doctrine and that this doctrine is the *real*, or at least the most important meaning of the Holy Writ (assuming that we distinguish between literal, allegorical, moral and metaphysical sense). And this is most difficult to accept both for historical and epistemological reasons. Myths are not 'really' theories. They are not translatable into a non-mythical tongue, supposedly apt to convey their genuine content. To believe that we can clarify this content or make it intelligible by this kind of translation is no more credible than to expect that we can hand over to someone the meaning of a musical work by telling them 'what it is about'. Myths would be dispensable if they had metaphysical equivalents. If they both express and conceal an ultimate reality this is because this reality is not expressible *in abstracto*, not reducible to any theoretical parlance.

It is plausible to think that various aspects of the ultimate reality are best expressed in religious worship and art – though not in the sense of a painter depicting the Absolute on a canvas or a priest explaining it in theoretically satisfactory categories. It is rather that what is nameless and not depictable may be hinted at – at least in intense religious and artistic acts – in such a manner that the hint conveys a feeling of understanding, a kind of momentary satisfaction which both is valid in cognitive terms and provides a certainty of being 'in touch with' or 'within' that which is more real than daily life reality. The satisfaction is bound to be momentary; it could assert itself as a permanent achievement only if its message were convertible into theoretical concepts which it is not by its very nature.

Within the language of the biblical myth in which God, though hidden, appears as a loving, if occasionally rather severe, protector, it is proper to say that his sadness in the face of our iniquities is no less real than his joy at the sight of the little good we prove to be capable of doing. If so, he is not a perfectly immutable Absolute, he is really growing through his creatures, he is, in other words, a historical god; it even appears that the very idea of the diffusion of divine love is not compatible with the absolute non-historicity and impassibility of the Creator, at least as long as those ideas of love and of impassibility retain the meaning we usually have in mind – and what other meaning could we construct?

If it were not the case that we *add* something to creation by trying to avoid evil and to spread love – however tiny the scale of our effort might be – then it would probably be wrong to say that we can 'do good' in a recognizable sense (assuming that goodness and being are co-extensive). To be sure, in terms of traditional wisdom whatever good there is in us, or is performed by us, is a reflex or an outflow of the divine goodness. But even then, it seems that by our choice and effort we make actual the goodness that was previously only potential and this amounts to saying that we *do* create something. If goodness is by definition always actual – which the dogma of the perfect actuality of God and of God's being the fullness of the good entails – the idea of human free choice is not tenable any longer.

Moreover, the very idea of creation becomes doubtful if those two dogmas are valid. The act of creation cannot add anything to the perfection and infinite goodness of God. By calling into existence the universe, time, space and mind, God does not change anything either in himself or in his relationships with his products; he is what he is, incorrigibly self-identical. Strictly speaking, no fiat of his can bring anything new into being, for the being is there, timelessly, eternally actual, infinite, consummated. The name 'God' becomes a sobriquet for the supreme Nothingness of the Absolute. Therefore, not only is evil nothing: good is equally nothing, as whatever good is, or might be, produced, does not augment the existing amount. This discloses another side of the *horror metaphysicus*: if God is the Absolute, there is no good and no evil and *a fortiori* no distinction between them.

In fact, not only the Bible – as well as sacred scriptures of other civilizations – offers us the image of God who is not a total plenitude of being but enjoys the good deeds of the denizens of this universe and thus presumably becomes richer as a result. This speculation about God, who, in the act of self-alienation or even self-mutilation is growing in the body of the universe and in the painful toil of human creatures, is not absent in Platonizing currents of Christian theology: in Scotus Erigena, in Eckhart, in Cusanus, in the German pantheists of the sixteenth and seventeenth centuries. It seems as if God, in this view, had to smash the impenetrable shell of his aseity, to break out of his unity, to expand and to venture into the universe in order to become what he was only potentially: a person. His self-supported subsistence 'before' time is then inaccessible to us, inexpressible and even indifferent; it can really be thrusted into the pale realm of negativity, of Nothingness. It is by becoming 'something' as a creator, lover and legislator, that God can be addressed or loved.

And is it not in keeping with common sense to admit with Hegel, that personal life (or self-consciousness) is conceivable only in contact and exchange – love or struggle, no matter – between persons, in other words, that there is no secluded self-contained personal mind? There is no way we could understand a divine person that would not face, and commune with, other person-like, and not necessarily divine, beings like ourselves.

From this theogonic perspective which, though repeatedly denied in words, has been a persistent temptation to neo-Platonic Christian thought, there is good reason to say that, by contributing to the goodness of the world and by shunning evil, we make the being grow. If we truly make a choice between good and evil, we make the being grow. This is what perhaps gives sense to the Heideggerian saying that 'man is the shepherd of the Being' – whether or not it was meant thus by Heidegger.

Does not such an admittedly heretical claim reveal human self-conceit? Does it not suggest that God, as it were, cannot take care of himself properly and that we have to defend him and help him? Perhaps. But this conceit, far from being self-serving or justifying our thirst for power, is compatible with the idea that goodness, albeit actuated by us, is not of our own making; nor does it suggest that we arbitrarily decide what is good or evil, it merely implies that it is up to us to choose between them.

91

We may presumptuously believe that the act of choosing is ours and humbly admit that we find the terms of the choice ready-made and have no power to define them according to our whims. If so, the conceit does not clash with the recommendable humility which Christian faith was supposed to teach us.

Within the same perspective, it is not preposterous to think that, by helping the being grow or weaken, we actually open the avenue to its understanding and thereby to the understanding of existence. This is again a genuinely Platonic and, at the same time, genuinely biblical insight which has been taken up and expressed on innumerable occasions in the history of both Christian and Jewish thought – not necessarily by thinkers who were of Platonist persuasions themselves (we find it very often in mystical literature; it was frequent among Erasmians). Variously articulated, this insight boils down to a fairly simple idea: there is no purely intellectual knowledge of God; insofar as we reach him only in speculation he remains an empty concept – not only useless in life, but void in cognitive terms as well; we know God to the extent of our piety: 'the Lord is nigh unto them that are of broken heart' (Ps. 34, 19), *timor Dei initium sapientae*, etc. Both the prophetic and didactic books of the Old Testament time and again identify wisdom with piety, righteousness, obedience and humility.

Here a brief historical restriction is not out of place, however. There is a certain ambiguity on this point in the history of the modern Roman Church. On the one hand, both the biblical legacy and the writings of many Fathers, Doctors, and recognized mystics – including St Bernard, St Bonaventure, Tauler, Thomas à Kempis, St John of the Cross, St Theresa – emphatically link our knowledge of God with our devotion, worship, faith, hope and charity.

This strongly suggests that purely speculative knowledge *in divinis* is not only worthless in terms of our salvation – which no Christian may deny, of course – but is no knowledge at all. This tenet, if taken seriously and unrestrictedly, would most likely make the entire natural theology and a good deal of the scholastic tradition fruitless and the time-honoured distinction between *scientia* and *sapientia* would not help much. The intransigent anti-philosophical trend, of which Lactantius' *De Falsa Sapientia* is a classic monument, has never entirely died out in Christian culture and St Paul's letters endow it with a permanent legitimacy. On the other hand, the purely intellectual path to God not only has not been denied by the Church but actually belongs to its dogmatic corpus. The defence of autonomy and value of speculative knowledge about God became more pressing in the disarray of the Counter-Reformation when it was imperative to attack Luther's and other reformers' contempt for natural theology and their concentration of all Christian virtues in the undifferentiated act of faith. It was no less important to leave room for the independent value of reason and knowledge than to defend the Church's legalistic tradition which was, after all, the unremovable pillar of its legitimacy. Somewhat similar problems were to emerge at the beginning of our century as a result of the modernist crisis.

But we do not need to bother now about the intricate vicissitudes of the devotion-versus-knowledge issue in the history of Christian dogma. The issue goes far beyond this specific story; that our knowledge of the absolute is an aspect of our spiritual life as a whole, in particular of the way we experience good and evil as our own good and evil, is a part of the Buddhist, Jewish, Christian and Platonic legacies. That in this experience we not only gain an access, however dim, however fleeting and 'unscientific', to the realm of the Being but enrich or impoverish this being itself, is not a well-codified and properly located part of any of those traditions but is scattered all over the history of civilizations, both in myth and in philosophical enquiry. In mythical languages, it is expressed as a belief that god rejoices or is saddened by our conduct. In metaphysical idiom the same insight may be voiced variously: by saying that God becomes 'something' from nothing in our souls; that the human race, as a vanguard of the universe, leads the whole of creation towards ultimate reconciliation with the Creator; that God, as *natura non naturata non naturans*, will absorb the world without destroying its variety; briefly that we provide God with a necessary aid in building the *Ultimum*, in God's becoming what he is; even that 'you are a thousand times more necessary to [God] than He is to you' (Meister Eckhart's saying in *Sermon on Luke*, 2.42); that despite the fact that the creatures have no being, they are a pure Nothingness and that the 'birth of God in the soul' is performed as a result of human self-induced passivity.

The belief that we get to know the Being by enlarging or injuring it in our good and evil acts is a very un-Kantian and non-pragmatist idea of the 'primacy of practical reason'. It is un-Kantian in that it does not infer the rules of practical reason from the universal norms of transcendental rationality wherein we all participate (ultimately, to Kant, the categorical imperative is valid because I cannot deny it without falling in self-contradiction). It is un-Kantian as well because it suggests that we get a glimpse of the Being from practically experiencing good and evil in us, rather than knowing it from rational attempts to reconcile the postulates of practical reason with empirical reality. And it is un-Kantian in that it does not offer any new philosophical solution to the old mystery, but only makes explicit a traditional belief. And it is most un-Kantian in the sense that acquaintance, however modest or immodest, with the Being, if it is achieved in this way, is not convertible into a generally valid theory. It depends on the experience in which people are initiated, to be sure, by education but to which a validating power is conferred only by personal encounter with ourselves as carriers of good and evil. It is not pragmatic either; neither does it dismiss metaphysical questioning on the criterion of utility nor is it ready to confer on this questioning a validity by applying this very criterion.

That the belief is traditional is indirectly borne out by the fact that the enfeebling of metaphysical faith and of religious worship is clearly, as a matter of historical experience, linked up with the gradual disappearance of the very notions of good and evil – whichever of those two acts of collapsing comes first; there is no need to prove how obsolete – for the time being, at least – how outmoded and meaningless those notions have become in our civilization.

If possible and plausible, this belief alters our hopeless hunt for that most elusive animal: existence as a primordial, irreducible act, not dependent on its relationship to any cognitive process, not empirically testable and supposedly given in an intellectual intuition of the absolute or in the existential intuition of *cogito*. The intuition of existence is not then grounded in our previous acquaintance with Absolute or *Cogito* but in a movement which, we feel, makes the Being grow or diminish as a result of the good or evil of our acts. The Being becomes intelligible within the self-perception of good and evil.

ALTER-EGO

If so, the *Cogito* is disposed of as well, next to the Absolute, as an ultimate foundation, at any rate in the Cartesian sense. It is not disposed of, however, exactly in the empiricist manner. The illusion of a direct ('unmediated') intuition of the 'self' is dispersed not by the simple fact that a pre-linguistic perception cannot be converted, unadulterated, into a theory, let alone into a theoretical foundation of knowledge; one may always plausibly argue that such a perception, though inexpressible, might still be valid, at least in the case under scrutiny, and give us an insight which – as I tried to suggest – is to us a paradigmatic case of 'existence'. The point is rather that what I have reached in the *Cogito* is not myself as a metaphysical entity; it is not open to me as a *de jure* self-contained universe.

By closing the ego as an epistemological ground beyond which there is nothing, Descartes actually made the empathic understanding of an alter-ego impossible; only the uncertain, indirect induction convinces me that there is an ego other than myself. And it is even most doubtful whether this inductive reasoning is sound on the assumption that no guesses by analogy can be legitimately made if an alter-ego is under the infallible protection of its own exclusivity, and impermeably sheltered from access.

The point is in fact trivial; it has been made on many occasions and by many people to quote whom would be a vain pageant of great names: to be a part of human community and to be involved in communication with others is an unremovable part of what is called improperly 'the I' (improperly, as 'I' is not a noun). My way of life, my acts and emotions are dependent on both what other people expect from me and the support they offer to me. This implies that whether or not I am really a part of the community depends on the degree to which I meet those expectations, and this implies that, in order to be that part, I have to see myself in terms of good and evil. The awareness of good and evil is therefore a condition which makes my being a part of the community possible and thus a condition of my continuous self-assertion of being myself. 'Ego' is made, among other things, of the awareness of good and evil. By blocking the ego, Cartesianism pushed it into nothingness. It is unblocked again and restored to reality when it is constituted in this awareness and thus in communication; this by no means implies that it is 'only' a part and has no ontological status of its own, that it is entirely derivative – both logically and ontologically – and secondary to the social 'whole' (as both Comte and Bradley believed); it may still be the case that by being a part it is not created but made actual.

To conceive of the 'self' as an ontologically autonomous entity that is made actual (or becomes a person) by communication within the realm of good and evil implies, in addition, that the self is located in a historically continous community and is aware, however indistinctly, of this belonging. In other words a community, in order to be real, has to include past and even hypothetical future generations, to live in a spiritual space in which the past is actual; a kind of communication with the ancestral spirits and the respect for the tombs have always been a natural expression of awareness that this spiritual space is real. That the reality of the self and the feeling of belonging to a historically defined community are linked up with each other is again borne out by the way they decline together in our civilization. The respect for the tombs, for the bodies of the dead and the awareness of living in a human city which stretches backwards and forward beyond the present generation fade away *pari passu* with the collapse of the reality of the self. The more historical community is perceived as unreal, the less 'I' am real myself. If this remark sounds Rousseauist, let it be so.

By trying to save the self and, at the same time, to rob it of its communal and historical dimensions, Descartes, whatever his intentions might have been, made 'me' as little real as the community, history, good or evil.

The upshot of this half-Cartesian and half-anti-Cartesian, half-Platonic and half-anti-Platonic discourse by no means aspires to offer new discoveries. It says:

There is no access to an epistemological absolute, and there is no privileged access to the absolute Being which might result in reliable theoretical knowledge (this last restriction is needed, as we may not a priori exclude the reality of mystical experience that provides some people with this privileged access; but their experience cannot be re-forged into a theory). This double denial does not need to end up with pragmatic nihilism; it is compatible with the belief that metaphysical and non-pragmatic insight is possible as a result of our living within the realm of good and evil and of experiencing good and evil as one's own.

But this denial explains why philosophy, like Peter Pan, never matures.

ON ALL POSSIBLE LANGUAGES (2)

And why should all this be believed? For such a belief there are obviously no grounds that belong to the commonly admitted rules of reasoning, which in turn derive their validity from a commonly accepted epistemological absolute, precisely because no such absolute is obtainable. Whether or not some of those traditional tenets which I tried to rephrase are credible, is a matter of our choice among all possible languages. This choice, however, is neither arbitrary nor guided by a previously acquired knowledge about the respective cognitive merits or superiority of one language over another; such a knowledge would require higher criteria of validity and thus would not escape the notorious sceptical circle. The choice is not arbitrary, though, it is not blind or random. In fact it consists in making explicit what we have already *known*.

In making one of all possible languages operational and intelligible – and thus in making a metaphysical or epistemological standpoint credible – we never start from the beginning. The choice among all possible languages is made not by God but by civilizations. Philosophies voice the aspirations and the choices of civilizations; this does not mean that philosophers are passive channels or phonographic instruments which civilizations employ to express themselves (as Hegelians occasionally seem to believe). By making a civilization explicit, they help it to expand and assert itself, not unlike all of us, who by an effort of expression, open new and unexpected avenues of our own evolution. To some extent, philosophies are compelled to make their own choices; by being limited and never impartial, they inevitably affirm some aspects of their civilization at the expense of others. Civilizations – at least those which need philosophy to express themselves and are known to us through this medium – are never perfectly coherent; if they were, they would be stuck in a stagnant self-complacency and propel themselves into destruction. The medium is therefore bound to distort the message. By being selective in revealing the hidden premises of a civilization and so providing it with a partial self-understanding and colouring this self-understanding with their personal biases, great philosophers, albeit unable simply to break out of their time, create points of discontinuity and push the 'spirit of the age' into a new direction; to what extent the results of this work are to be seen as a continuation or as a rupture in the history of culture is usually uncertain, even after centuries.

Willingly or unwillingly, philosophers, when they try to utter the unspelt aspirations of their age and draw, at the same time, from their personal resources, create, or co-create or perhaps actuate new languages. Some of those languages prove to be stillborn and quickly sink into oblivion. Some remain and strike roots in the soil of culture but then they usually are not immediately, naturally convincing or even intelligible. More often than not to understand a new language of philosophy is a matter of spiritual conversion: the act of understanding and believing are undistinguishable, perhaps even the latter precedes the former.

Let us look at the first sentence of Wittgenstein's *Tractatus* – no less revealing, though incomparably less frequently quoted than the famous last sentence. It reads: 'perhaps this book will be understood only by someone who has himself already had the thoughts that are expressed in it – or at least similar thoughts.' To say this amounts to repeating '*credo ut intelligam*' (the saying does not square properly, for that matter, with Wittgenstein's belief to have offered a perfectly clear final solution, definitive truth etc.). And indeed, more often than not, this principle works in philosophy no less than in religious faith: if we set aside the positivist and materialist anti-philosophies, a philosophy becomes intelligible through a kind of initiation which is not preceded by an act of intellectual understanding; we understand it in the very act of acceptance which might or might not agree with the thinker's self-interpretation. That is why philosophers so often complain about being misunderstood. According to Wittgenstein, Bertrand Russell failed to grasp the meaning of the *Tractatus*. Hegel is said to have said that only one man had understood him and he had understood him wrongly. Some scholars argue that Aristotle, after two decades in the Academy, failed to understand Plato who in turn, having spent several years in the company of Socrates, did not know what the teaching of the master was about. Avicenna had perused *Metaphysics* forty times before he began to comprehend its sense, Jansenius had to read the whole of St Augustine ten times and his works on grace thirty times before he dared compose his voluminous heretical treatise. James misrepresented Peirce no less than Sartre did Heidegger, etc.

The vicissitudes of philosophy teem with such stories which at first glance seem to give an unflattering testimony to philosophy's bold claims to truth and precision, but perhaps, on closer inspection, simply confirm the principle just mentioned. There is no all-encompassing language; and there are as many possible languages as there are possible angles from which the Being and Nothingness can be observed, which means: indefinitely many. And there is no angle that opens all perspectives simultaneously unless it coincides with the divine eye. Sometimes we can shift from one angle to another without forgetting our previous sight and therefore we are able to perceive the truth of several metaphysical perspectives which, once reduced to a supposedly common language, collide with each other. But more often we stick by one observation point, after having been pushed there both by the compelling forces of our civilization and by our mental preferences, our temptations and desires. Then I and my neighbour really perceive different things.

It has been the contention of a number of philosophers and linguists that the identification of objects both in language and in perception is guided by practical considerations, by needs, will, in brief by an interest of a kind, whether species-related – and thus universally human – or specific to a particular society, civilization or even individual. This seems incompatible with the belief that there must be simple objects unless this belief is seen as one of many world images, all of them equally valid. The same principle of plurality of equipollent views is *a fortiori* applicable to the language of metaphysics.

But then we are back at the very beginning of our horror. How can I stick to a particular language (or to an angle from which the world is seen, or to a rule of interpretation of the whole of experience) and not endow it with a privileged cognitive prowess? And if I pretend to have at my disposal a higher, or even an absolute, language, then it either would be suitable only to talk about other languages but not about the reality they refer to, or it would be a standard language of which the other are incomplete dialects. If it is the latter, it is really a divine absolute tongue, embracing all conceivable points of view. Such a tongue is impossible; even God, when talking through the mouth of a prophet, has to translate himself into a human language; the translation is admittedly distorting and we have no access to the original. If it is the former, my particular language (of the first degree, the language of things), may not indeed make claims to any privileged position, but I would not be capable of explaining *in it* the absence of this privileged position: to do that I should abandon my language and turn to a super (or meta) language in which my particular position is inexpressible.

In other words: when I am saying magnanimously 'all metaphysical positions are equally good', I do not take any position, I just express the principle of tolerance, which, however laudable, is formal and will never produce or even encourage any metaphysical idea. When I am trying to keep this principle in mind and combine it with my particular position, I am incoherent, because then I say 'my position is as good as any other, even though it is incompatible with them'. By doing that I cannot intelligibly explain in what sense this is *my* position in contrast to others'. Tolerant generosity does not offer an escape from the self-reference paradox, alas.

Polish logician and painter, Leon Chwistek published in 1921 a book, *The Plurality of Reality*, in which he suggested that there are four kinds of mutually independent, and presumably non-interfering, realities: of things, as they are discerned by common sense; of physical science; of impressions; and of imagination. They are artistically expressed as primitivist, naturalist, impressionist, and futurist painting respectively. But then, he argued, this plurality justifies an indefinite number of equally valid world views, none of them provable, but each acceptable on the condition that it does not try to establish a monopoly of truth for itself. Various answers to traditional questions like freedom of will, mind and body, objectivity of values, become permissible once they are limited to one or some of the four realities.

The theory of many - however identified - realities, even if created perhaps in this case as a metaphysical explanation of painting, is a plausible and tempting image of the universe, but as soon as it is supposed to be an epistemological proposal, it cannot - either in Chwistek's case or in that of William James - cope with this same obstacle: how to assert the superiority of a theory of being in the same language in which this very theory is phrased? Shall we state that ultimately the saying 'everything is necessary' is as valid as 'nothing is necessary except for logical relationships', and the doctrine 'the word "I" has no reference' is no less true than the doctrine 'whatever has a reference is relative to the "I"'? Shall we one day see a genius who has proved (and not just said) that from the higher standpoint St Augustine, Spinoza, Hume, Kant and Hegel either said the same thing or at least expressed perfectly compatible visions of reality, as it can be seen from different angles? A tsadik, quoted by Martin Buber, said that all the sayings, contradicting each other, of Jewish sages are true in heaven, as all truths are in heaven united. We shall see.

If layers of reality, independent from one another, require, in order to be described, independent languages, then there is a strong suggestion that those languages are totally untranslatable, and, if so, there is indeed a good reason to argue that various world views can co-exist in perfect mutual indifference: they cannot be confronted with, or contradict, each other. And this very saying that 'they cannot be confronted, etc.' is expressed in a higher language which in turn is metaphysically void. Then we are back in the same quandary: *either* we limit ourselves to this higher language and make our verdicts irrelevant to the real worries that philosophy makes its living from, *or* we commit ourselves to a particular metaphysical outlook and declare that this outlook, being closed, can never be harmonized with, or contradict, its supposed rivals, and this self-interpretation again makes our outlook irrelevant to the real worries that philosophy makes its living from.

There is a reason why metaphysical ecumenism is less reliable and logically more precarious than the religious one.

When the romantics and many of their followers in our century – whether religious sages or scholars – repeated, in various versions, William Blake's saying 'all religions are one', they had in mind one of two possible tenets and sometimes were guilty of not distinguishing them clearly from each other.

'All religions are one' might mean that there is a stock, however limited, of identifiable and expressible important beliefs which are common to all religions and in which all worshippers recognize themselves. This view, whether right or wrong, implies that religion is a collection of statements of which some really do matter and some do not and that those which matter are included in all the known 'systems of beliefs'.

The same saying might mean, on the other hand, that all religions are culture-bound expressions of fundamentally the same human experience which, however, can never be uttered in its uncontaminated, original quality, but is disguised in a variety of rites, myths, dogmas, taboos and norms, none of which may aspire to enjoy exclusive validity. The core of religious life is indeed the same, but it is not a core consisting of doctrinal assertions which could be distilled from the countless forms of worship as their unifying principle; once dressed in words this core cannot but belong to a particular civilization; people from various epochs and various cultural territories may share the same experience but every time they try to give it the proper 'theoretical' shape they fail: people from other civilizations do not recognize themselves in this reconstruction

The first of the two versions is almost certainly wrong. It is most unlikely that one could find a universal dogma of all religions, effectively recognized in all of them, unless it be a vague generality, bordering on meaninglessness, or an uncontroversial platitude. The second version is much more plausible, if not as an empirically or historically provable theory, then as a fertile hermeneutic rule. At any rate it helps us look for and find a community of meaning in disparate and unconnected religious life forms, without pretending that the common meaning, thus discovered, could replace the actual, historically shaped worship. It does not even exclude the prospect, however unlikely and remote, of a universally human religious community which has found a common language of worship; even then, however, the expression of religious experience would still be symbolic and historically relative, for the gap between the actual experience and all our symbolic forms, no matter how rich and how widely spread, remains unbridgeable.

Philosophical ecumenism does not suffer from this ambiguity because philosophy's vocation is to be articulated in language only and to offer arguments; it may not refer – or so it seems – to an inexpressible experience in search of its common gist; if it existed, such a gist would have a propositional form, pretending to be logically satisfying. And it will not be excavated from under the depressingly huge piles of words which philosophy is made of. It could not even be reduced to an uncontroversial banality, as there is no banality so banal that its meaning would not be occasionally challenged or contested by philosophers. Therefore it is likely – if we trust the guidance of historical experience – that mutually un-understandable and incongruous idioms will compete with each other. Among all possible, infinitely numerous, languages, none is probably all-encompassing save the *lingua incognita Dei*.

Even tolerance is easier and better justifiable – *de jure*, not as a matter of historical record, of course – in religious worship than in philosophy because, apart from having various non-verbal means of expression, religious worship includes the implicit, and very frequently explicit, admission that the human tongue is inept and defective when speaking about the unspeakable. For that reason it is potentially more natural to accept the variety of religious idioms, all of them by necessity clumsy. In actual fact it is more difficult, because not only verbally shaped beliefs, but rituals and customs as well, tend to assert their claims to absolute validity, and people have reason to take it for granted that much more is at stake when religious issues are debated (one of the crucial bones of contention in the history of the eastern schism which sealed the great split in the Christian church with enormous consequences for the future of civilization, was the question of whether leavened or unleavened bread should be used in the Holy Communion). Philosophy, however, makes claims not only to the truth but to the literal truth; its pronouncements as a rule are true as they stand, without allowances being made for the inherent inadequacy of the word. A philosopher normally assumes that whatever another one has said is, if meaningful at all, translatable in his own slang; the untranslatability, usually not admitted, works nonetheless as a safety-net in conflicts ('your criticism proves that you misunderstood me completely') unless they occur within the same linguistic convention and refer to specific, limited points.

Great philosophers, who mark points of discontinuity in the spiritual itinerary of mankind, start from a place that has not yet been discovered, from what had been a blank spot of the map of the Mind. They are compelled to give a name to this spot from where they see the surrounding landscape differently. They create a virgin tongue and no insurmountable obstacles stand in the way of those listeners who want to set foot on the same place, see the same sight, and assimilate the same linguistic tools to depict it. Usually this is not easy, though, as we naturally try to translate foreign texts into a familiar dialect – and we miss the meaning. Any example will do. When reading Heidegger's words: *Das Sosein des Daseins ist die Sorge*, an analytical philosopher tends to think that what the German seeks to state is that people often worry about various things – a moderately enlightening remark. We certainly may try a less trivial translation, but, having reached a certain degree of intimacy with the new tongue, we will most likely come to the conclusion that the best way to say what Heidegger sought to say is the way he said it. We have become used to some untranslatable concepts of oriental philosophy like Tao or Atman and those who (like the author) cannot read Chinese and Sanskrit texts in the original will probably never grasp their full meaning, but the confusion of tongues in philosophy is different from, and more troublesome than, ethnic diversity. Both Indian wisdom and, in the European tradition, neo-Platonic philosophy inhabit a spiritual territory where it is assumed that the Whole can be contained in a part and if we start from the certainty that this is self-evidently impossible because the terrestial globe cannot be packed into a chocolate box, we have to give up the effort of understanding and leave this entire tradition in the pit of the superstitious past where it presumably belongs. What shall we do with the saying of some Buddhist sages that *samsara* and *nirvana* are the same? Or, with Sankara's tenet: 'As I am devoid of life principle, I do not act. Being without intellect, I am not a knower. Therefore I have neither knowledge nor nescience, having the light of pure consciousness only?' (*A Thousand Teachings*, chapter 13, translated by

Sengaku Mayeda). And yet those who have communed for some time with Buddhist and Hindu thought find nothing incomprehensible in such sayings; they might instead make little sense, for instance, of the Jewish image of God.

The point of new tongues is not really the fabrication of neologisms, an art in which the Germans have excelled for centuries; great philosophers who solely employed the existing lexical resources produced new tongues, too, by compelling old words to depict new sides.

A digression: one of my teachers of logic, Professor Kazimierz Ajdukiewicz, elaborated a formal theory of closed and coherent, mutually totally untranslatable languages (published as a series of articles in *Erkenntnis* in the late 1930s). Many years later I, as a young omniscient student (I was soon to lose both those virtues, alas), attacked this theory and pointed out that its author was unable to find a single example to support it. I now think that what comes closest to an example of such languages is self-contained philosophical 'systems' as well as expressions of religious worship.

How did the confusion of tongues come about? The biblical story (Gen. XI, 1–9) deals, of course, with ethnic tongues of which diversity seems to be both the divinely inflicted punishment for human hubris and the practical measure applied by God to prevent this supercilious race from doing whatever they might think of. The standard Christian exegesis connects this fateful event with the illapse of the Holy Ghost who bestowed the gift of tongues on the Apostles (Acts, II, 1–13), thus restoring, thanks to Jesus Christ's sacrifice, the unity which mankind had lost by its own fault. Philo of Alexandria in a treatise on the subject attempted another, somewhat risky, allegorical interpretation. Since people more often than not were wicked and used their freedom for doing evil (pious people should pray that their designs and intentions fizzle out) God, by preventing them from carrying out their wishes, simply wanted to lower the amount of evil and confused their tongues for that purpose. However 'confusion' is not separation – otherwise the latter word would have been used by Moses. The confusion occurs when various ingredients are so mixed together that they cannot be separated again and none of their previous properties remain but new qualities are created instead. The unique tongue from before the construction of Babel stands for the collection of human depravities out of which God made a compound in order to render each of them helpless in destroying the good (*De Confusione linguarum*, XXXVII–XXXVIII).

As an exegetical exercise Philo's allegory does not sound convincing. It has been recalled here in order to make a quasi-theological suggestion, purporting to explain the confusion of philosophical tongues and based on the confusion between both meanings of 'confusion' – the Christian one and Philo's chemical one.

As long as people dwell in a relatively stable and mythologically ordered universe, both the meaning of current events and the unity of the world, vaulted by a history of creation, are clear and immune to scrutiny. The order is both physical and moral and thus the question of how to distinguish the real from the unreal, or the good from the evil has no room where it might appear. The original sin of philosophy (or of the Enlightenment) consisted in having forsaken this order to construct another one, rooted in Reason alone. This amounted to trying to usurp for themselves divine rights or to building a tower that would reach heaven. Let us remember that the tower of Babel was supposed to prevent people from being dispersed on earth and so promote human unity; but the effect belied the intentions. Philosophy was to discover, on a deserted field, the meaning of the world and its unity; the tools for this task were the senses and logic. Like mythologies, philosophy assumed that things are not what they seem to be in our eyes, that the world calls for explanation and that, to make it intelligible, its unity – both of its stuff and of its historical origin – has to be found; unlike mythologies, it assumed that we do not find the meaning ready-made but that Reason is capable of reconstructing it. Therefore, philosophy was naturally led to making the distinction between efficient and final causes, i.e. between what is meaningless and what is meaningful in events, as well as a distinction between the physical and moral order. None of them could serve as a support for another and they had to be investigated and rebuilt separately.

The confusion of tongues was then inevitable. In the slow progress the criteria were codified to which an agreement within Reason was feasible and the set of these criteria was to be called science. In the area which philosophy inherited from the core of mythology – an all-encompassing world of meaning – no such criteria were attainable and this area was eventually to establish itself as philosophy proper. Philosophy is by definition a territory of the confusion of tongues, that is to say, where no agreement is attainable as to the criteria of validity. To be sure, a good deal of philosophy is devoted to the task of proving that philosophy, as defined by its original ambition, is impossible, since commonly acceptable criteria cannot validate it, or, to put it simply, that the search for 'meaning' is vain because meaning is not visible in the world (not unlike the atheist criticism of religion which boils down to the observation that 'nobody has ever seen God' – which is both true and attested by the Bible). And between science and philosophy there is a grey area consisting of a number of half-sciences.

So far, the story of the disaster of Babel, at least in its ostensible sense, has been borne out: the confusion of tongues in philosophy is a punishment for the very act of inventing philosophy, or the revenge of mythology on the enlightenment for the latter's arrogant attempt to demolish the former. Philosophy, on the one hand, has boasted of being the truth-seeker *par excellence* but, on the other hand, has had the monopolistic right to establish what the truth verily is. If it took this right seriously, it placed itself in the enviable position of a judge who is bound neither by a legal code nor by the stock of precedents: he has simply the power to issue the universally valid law *ad hoc* and then to declare that any particular verdict he makes is lawful and derives its validity from the universal code. A price had to be paid for this royal privilege, however, and it consisted in that anybody could make claim to it. On this assumption, the concept of truth, and consequently truth itself, could become the exclusive property of anybody who wanted to possess it. The rightful claim to exclusive ownership of the same thing by many would-be owners inevitably resulted in many equally valid but untranslatable languages, as no Supreme Court was there to make one claim better grounded than any other. *Horror metaphysicus*, and the spectre of never-ending uncertainty, were bound to appear.

If philosophy, however, instead of building the concept of truth according to its free imagination, takes it from sciences and tries to assert itself as one of their branches, it cuts itself off from its roots and its original calling, thus risking becoming an uninteresting *divertissement*, of little relevance to the real worries – whether scientific, moral, or social – of civilization. But confusion in the sense of 'separation' has a side which makes it similar to Philo's confusion conceived of as a chemical compound. Despite the dispersion of tongues, philosophy succeeded in marking, however imprecisely, a realm of cultural life, which, though often scoffed at, enjoys a wobbly legitimacy and absorbs various mutually unintelligible idioms. Not unlike human sins and defects that limit and check each other according to God's cunning design in Philo's description, those idioms occupy their respective niches in culture and prevent each other from becoming unrestrictedly dominant. In this realm the pentecostal miracle, if possible, still lies ahead.

READING THE WORLD

German thinkers have been teaching us for quite a long time that the human race has a natural 'hermeneutic' orientation, that is to say it tries, almost instinctively, to discover the meaning in everything it happens to experience. To find a 'meaning' means in this context more than to identify objects, events and concepts in terms of human – personal or universal – needs, aspirations, uses and dangers; in thus talking about 'meaning' or 'meaning-grasping' we do not go beyond the purely naturalist or functionalist anthropology. The 'meaning' which the hermeneutics speak of seems to suggest much more. First of all, it is trivial and uncontroversial – setting aside the die-hard behaviourists – that we naturally (that is: as a matter of lasting cultural habit) endow with an additional meaning those human activities and products which might seem to be no more than an extension of animal behaviour. We know from experience that love is more than the reproductive drive and that the idea of home carries a meaning that is not included in the sheer concept of a shelter. We believe that our knowledge is not only a device whereby we increase the chances of the survival of the species but pretends to be a quest for truth, a good we hold dear apart from the practical benefits the growth of knowledge might bring. We believe that a human person is valuable in itself and not merely as a traveller, hired by Nature, to produce the sperms or eggs that are necessary for the continuation of the species. We know that relationships between parents and children go far beyond the arrangement of Nature on whose order the begetters care about their offspring. We feel that our language is more than a collection of signals we exchange for practical purposes, that it is a form of soul and it creates a community which is an ontological entity in its own right, and not just an instrument of survival. Moreover, we believe that as a result of this new meaning, all the characteristics we share with animals change their meaning as well, once they appear to us in this contrasting pair 'animal human', in other words that there is nothing non-human in us: both the whore and the Holy Virgin are uniquely human; so are both the awareness of being mortal and the awareness of being immortal. Briefly, we naturally believe in the discontinuity of the life tree or in a separate fiat which brought us into existence.

So conceived 'meaning' seems to refer to the entire exclusively human spiritual reality which is neither restricted to psychological facts, i.e., to what is actually experienced, nor reducible to pre-human sides of our life. 'Meaningful' is what makes a part, or can be described in terms of, this reality which Hegel was probably the first to

114

have identified as a separate realm of being. Insofar as it wants to examine such a 'meaning', hermeneutics is not ontologically neutral: it is bound to assume, implicitly at least, that the Mind can be understood or can reveal 'meaning' because it is really endowed with meaning, as distinct from conscious intentions of people who left the materialized traces of their life in the form of various artefacts, such as tools, buildings, works of art, spoken words, bills, scientific theories, mythological stories, broken bones of their neighbours and the like.

If, however, the understanding (i.e. *Verstehen*) refers to '*meaning*' as conveyed by intentions of individuals who were authors of those artefacts and if it consists in attempts to re-enact those intentions in an empathic insight (Dilthey might have occasionally prompted his readers to this assumption; not so Gadamer), no special ontology of the 'objective Mind' is necessary but the prospects of the search for meaning become dubious. We may claim to be capable of understanding, say, Zurbaran's painting *St Bonaventure on his Deathbed* or Beethoven's Violin Concerto, because we have our share in universally human, and not historically limited, aspirations, fears, yearnings, joys and worries, and because we know something of the specific cultural setting of which those works are fragments; but we clearly cannot substitute Zurbaran's or Beethoven's minds for our own and recreate or re-experience their respective intentions and feelings.

'Meaning' which is not psychologically definable but is supposed to be really included in human activity and its products, or to be a speech of the Mind, should be a speech of human history as well; in other words, human history, on this assumption, becomes intelligible *per se*, not only in the sense that the motivations of its actors are intelligible. And what is it to understand history, if it is neither to understand the motivations of individuals nor to disclose, as Bossuet did, a well devised divine plan which the course of human affairs through centuries both reveals and conceals? Certainly it is not just to notice some quantifiable tendencies like the fact that, if a sufficiently large span of time is considered, people on average tend to live longer and are able to employ more and more natural energies for their purposes; such facts are just facts, not meanings. Nor do we mean the examination of causal relationships. Where then is the target of this quest for a non-theological and non-psychological understanding? The assumption apparently is that we understand the historical process as an unfolding of a Hegelian universal Mind which is neither divine nor individual-human, has no identifiable self-awareness and no transcendent means of subsistence, but paves the way for an indefinable goal by the intermediary of human efforts and desires; unlike Hegel, hermeneutics does not need, indeed, to track down the ultimate goal of the Mind and therefore it may glory in being metaphysically neutral. Yet it is not. To assume, even implicitly, an impersonal Mind, immanent in history, a Mind of which human individuals are unconscious aids (if not serfs) and which, in an apparently erratic manner, reveals its will, is to move on the soil of metaphysics.

This by no means entails that the hermeneutic enquiry is wrong or fruitless. It does entail, however, that, unlike science, it cannot appeal to commonly admissible criteria of validity.

Moreover, it does not shun further expansion; it is ready to stretch the meaning onto non-man-made nature as well. Gadamer (in his essay on aesthetics and hermeneutics) quotes Goethe's words: 'everything is a symbol' and explains that in the experience of both history and nature we listen to a language. That everything can be thus listened to does not imply that in the act of listening we get to know what the Being is but only how it appears in human understanding; and indeed, there is nothing meaningless for us.

This explanation is somewhat elusive. That every experience and every object encountered can be of relevance to human life is not a matter of dispute as long as we have in mind either possible practical benefit or aesthetic reaction (a digression: the very fact that we are able to react aesthetically to nature is astonishing, and, in terms of a philosophy which relates all human experience to cultural 'wholes', it has to be considered parasitic on the perception of art, or even altogether dismissed – as in Croce). Whatever there is within the horizon of our perception and thought is being absorbed as a part of the world we inhabit and try to tame. But do we simply create this meaning by decree, by relating the world to our practical, cognitive and aesthetic aspirations or do we discover it? Or both? My guess is that in the perspective of hermeneutics the answer is: both. If so, the meaning is neither freely produced by us nor simply ready-made, embedded in nature or history, and awaiting a discoverer. It is rather that the meaning-generating Mind is being made actual in the very process of revealing itself to our mind, or that the meaning-endowed Being is 'becoming what it is' thanks to human understanding of what it is. This comes closer to the idea, discussed above, of the 'historical God'.

I am not entirely confident that this is a perfectly accurate reconstruction of the intended metaphysical background of hermeneutics. But the point here is not what is the correct reading of a philosopher; it is rather to

117

say that if hermeneutics consists in searching for 'meaning' beyond the intentions of individuals, if it wants to embrace historical processes and the entire realm of nature, it may not dispense with belief in a Mind which is not ours, even if it is not necessarily the fully-fledged, perfectly self-conscious, divine ruler of the universe or the timeless Absolute.

The alternative to this belief is a consistently scientistic world-image which implies or explicitly states that 'to be' is pointless, that neither the universe nor life nor history have any purpose and that there is no meaning apart from human intentions. Piaget, for instance, explains that the search for final causes corresponds to the childish stage of human development; it is little children who keep asking 'who made it?' (this mountain or that waterfall); but they grow up and stop asking, and so does mankind. Jacques Monod's renowed opus, *Hazard and Necessity* is an attempt to convince us that life and human forms of life are due to chance in the strongest possible sense of this word.

And yet, we do not grow up in the sense Piaget wishes us to; and if children ask such questions this is probably because it is natural for us to do so. The growth of the Enlightenment culminates precisely in this injunction: 'stop asking such questions'. But the Enlightenment, as Gadamer aptly observes, is merely a stage in our destiny.

We have never stopped and most likely never will stop asking such questions. We shall never get rid of the temptation to perceive the universe as a secret script to which we stubbornly try to find the clue. And why, indeed, should we get rid of this temptation which proved to be the most fruitful source in all civilizations except our own (or, at least, its dominant trend)? And where does the supreme validity of the verdict which forbids us this search come from? Only from the fact that this civilization - ours - which to a large extent has got rid of this search proved immensely successful in some respects; but it has failed pathetically in many others.

One may ask: assuming that the universe is indeed a secret script of the gods and that it does convey a message to us, why should this message not be written in plain words rather than in hieroglyphs whose decoding is discouragingly arduous and, above all, never results in certainty?

This question is futile for two independent reasons. Firstly, it assumes that we do know or can imagine what the universe would be like if its message and meaning were clearly readable and unambiguously displayed before our eyes. But we do not know that and we lack this kind of imagination. Secondly, it is possible that if we knew why the message is hidden (or even partially hidden) it would not be hidden any longer; in other words that concealment of the reasons why it is hidden is unavoidably a part of its being hidden.

Some people make claims to be capable of breaking - in part, of course, never fully - this perplexing cipher, and this not necessarily thanks to a gnostic initiation, a privileged access to an esoteric treasure of knowledge; they rather claim to have taken a special spiritual attitude, opened themselves to the voice of the meaning-carrying Mind; and they say that this tuning-in is universally accessible. They might be wrong, no doubt, and those of us who do not hear this voice cannot be convinced on the ground they have chosen as their own; those who hear are then classified as victims of delusions. But if they are right and if the voice is audible to anybody who really wants to hear, the question, 'why is the message hidden?' is wrongly asked.

And is it not a plausible suspicion that if 'to be' were pointless and the universe void of meaning, we would never have achieved not only the ability to imagine otherwise but even the ability to think precisely this: that 'to be' is indeed pointless and the universe void of meaning?

Index of Names